CLEM SEECHARAN

INDIA AND THE SHAPING
OF THE INDO-GUYANESE IMAGINATION
1890s - 1920s

PEEPAL TREE

First published in Great Britain in 1993
by the Centre for Research in Asian Migration
The University of Warwick
and Peepal Tree Books
17 King's Avenue
Leeds LS6 1QS
England

ISBN 0 948833 61 0

Dr. William Hewley Wharton:
the first Indo-Guyanese to study at a British university

Joseph Ruhomon:
the first Indian intellectual in Guyana

Pandit Ramsaroop, M.B.E.
founder of the Hindu Society 1922;
'indefatigable worker for the poor'

Acknowledgements

I wish to thank my wife, Chris Vaughan, for her critical comments, material support, and patience. I am also grateful to David Dabydeen for his continuing confidence in me; Marjorie Davies for typing several drafts of this effort; and Jeremy Poynting for publishing it.

Clem Seecharan
Centre for Research in
Asian Migration,
University of Warwick

The Centre for Research in Asian Migration is most grateful to Messrs. Vipin and Anant Shah (The M.P. Shah Charitable Foundation), and Mr. Dan Gidwaney (Accountancy Tutors Ltd.) for their sponsorship of this publication.

To my friends
Ole Bai (Basdeo Adheen)
1931-1990
and Sister Ram
1933-1993

CONTENTS

... the history of India is a longer history than the history of Europe, and creeds and laws and words and traditions had been growing and changing and decaying on the borders of the Sarasvati and the Ganges, before the Saxons had reached the borders of the Elbe and their descendants had settled on the coast of Kent. There may have been less change in India than in Europe, but there has been considerable change in India too.

F. Max Müller, 'Caste' [1858], in *Chips from a German Workshop, Vol. II*, (London: Longmans, Green, and Co., 1880), pp. 302-303.

By the end of the [nineteenth] century, Hinduism stood erect before the world, fully conscious of its own greatness and powers and ready, if necessary, to challenge the teachings of rival religions. The sense of Hindu greatness was also awakened and fortified by the recovery of Indian history. By slow and patient labour European scholars had begun to reconstruct the lost story of India's greatness... Gradually the Hindu awoke to the fact that his was not a race whose destiny it was to be conquered by foreign people, but one which through many centuries had to its credit great achievements in every sphere.

K.M. Panikkar, *A Survey of Indian History*, (London: Asia Publishing House, 1956 [1947]), p. 217.

To India

Save Greece, like thee, what other land
Could dare produce two epics grand
    That yet would charm the ages?
Except those classic-words were sound,
Containing thoughts both wise, profound,
Could they their readers still astound —
    Those deep, immortal pages?

W.W. Persaud [Indo-Guyanese] in *Anthology of Local Indian Verse*, C.E.J. Ramcharitar-Lalla, (ed.), (Georgetown: 'The Argosy' Co., 1934), p. 22.

I

INTELLECTUAL PROMPTINGS: EUROPEAN SCHOLARSHIP AND THE HINDU RENEWAL IN INDIA

...I ask you...not to forget that you are Indians, that you are the sons, like I am, of a country with a very great past; of a country whose civilisation is one of the oldest in the world (cheers); of a country which has produced one of the greatest founders of religion — ... the Great Gautama Buddha; a country which has produced some architecture and magnificence of buildings, which are the envy of the world; a country which has a very brilliant literature and drama; a country which has inculcated, in its best day, a spirit of humanity and of tolerance. I ask you never to forget such a country, and I ask you again never to forget that you are that country's sons.

Kunwar Maharaj Singh (Colonisation Delegate from India), 'Address to the British Guiana East Indian Association', November 1925... quoted in 'Memorandum of East Indian Intelligentsia of British Guiana to the Members of the Royal Commission, 1939' — C. O. 950/941 (West India Royal Commission, 1938–39. Written Evidence, Vol. 3).

The intellectual life of India in the 7th and 6th centuries B. C. was as vigorous and pulsating as the jungle after the rains.

A. L. Basham, *The Wonder that was India* (London: Fontana/Collins, 1971 [1954]), p. 251.

We are an old race, or rather an odd mixture of many races, and our racial memories go back to the dawn of history.

J. Nehru, *The Discovery of India* (London: Meridian Books, 1956 [1946]), p. 42.

The rise of Indian self-confidence and assertiveness in British Guiana, especially from the 1920s, cannot be comprehended in isolation from the positive image of the ancestral homeland which took shape from the 1890s. The retention of Hinduism and Islam, in an alien environment rampant with Christian proselytisers, was a solid affirmation of India and her ancient values. This was evident even among illiterate men and women in the colony. Because many retained no direct contact with India, their conception of it tended to assume mythical dimensions: the heroic, ethereal, idyllic Aryan India of the Hindu epics — a Golden Age — lodged permanently in the Indo-Guyanese psyche. This inviolable, surreal India was a potent, malleable instrument of self-preservation, of racial dignity, in a society where few, if any, dared to challenge European definitions of the human condition.

Central to Indian cultural resistance in British Guiana was their identity with the heartland of Hinduism, the land of the Hindu epic, the *Ramayana*[1]: 85 per cent of the indentured labourers to the colony originated in the eastern districts of the United Provinces and the western districts of Bihar. To these simple folk, it was enough that their culture had spawned a massive body of religious literature. The fact that it was contained in books, was magical: this spoke of their own high achievement, in a European idiom. Moreover, the pervasive tendency for Christians to calumniate the Indians' rich, ancient, religious heritage, strengthened their resolve to perpetuate the rites and rituals of the 'motherland'. In the early 1880s, the Rev. H. V. P. Bronkhurst, Methodist missionary to the Indians in British Guiana, acknowledged that after two decades, his message had lodged on stony ground. The Hindus were, indeed, unrepentant; they were practising their own religion with undiminished tenacity. Bronkhurst observed, despairingly:

> ...their religion exercises a prodigious influence over the people. Blind adherence is paid to this cursed system. The Coolies deem it as perilous to forsake their religion as for a locomotive to quit the line. Whatever may be thought by others of the absurdity of the thing, they nevertheless sincerely believe in the divinity of a dumb idol. The evidence of their senses goes for nothing in the face of time-honoured and hoary tradition. [2]

This strident, jarring intolerance must have galled even Christian converts among Indo-Guyanese. And the lumping of all Indians as 'coolies', a pejorative that spoke of menial jobbing and myriad associations of inferiority, as Edgar Mittelholzer recalls, 'whether they were labourers or eventually became doctors or barristers or civil servants'[3], must have exacerbated the pain, prolonged the shame, among educated Indians. By the 1890s, however, a few literate, inquisitive Indians in British Guiana could take pride in claiming aspects of their ancient, ancestral culture. Their literacy in English, their exposure to the civilised, liberal strain in western thought — to philosophical rationalism with its remorseless pursuit of freedom and personal liberty and responsibility — bred a critical perspective. This fed a curiosity for self-knowledge, of ancient Indian history and culture.

It is noteworthy that the latter half of the nineteenth century, in India, was characterised by a virtual Hindu renaissance, centred primarily on Bengal, but with all-India resonances. This process stemmed exclusively from the pioneering work of European scholars, who, from the late eighteenth century, discovered the richness and sophistication of ancient Hindu civilisation: its art, sculpture, cave paintings, architectural splendour, and its enviable, massive corpus of literature in Sanskrit. It was under the liberal Governor-General of Bengal, Warren Hastings (1732-1818), that a body of eminent scholars/administrators, based in Calcutta, tackled the intellectual heritage of Aryan India. The pioneer was Sir William Jones (1746-1794), who founded the Asiatic Society of Bengal in 1784; and made English translations of Kalidasa's *Shakuntala,* a masterpiece of Sanskrit drama, in 1789;[4] the *Gita Govinda* in 1792; and the law-book of Manu, *Institutes of Hindoo Law,* published in 1794.

Jones also founded a journal, *Asiatic Researches,* in July 1789; thus providing a forum for scholarly studies in Sanskrit grammar, philosophy, and the immense literature of the Vedic period, undertaken by the distinguished Indologists, Henry Colebrook (1767-1837), Nathaniel Halhed, Charles Wilkins (1749-1836), William Hunter, and others. It was Warren Hastings's contention that the British would always be treated as aliens unless they were able to comprehend the philosophical and religious promptings of Indian attitudes. [5] So there was a pragmatic, practical basis for his promotion of Indology (see Appendix 1); but he, unwittingly, unleashed infinitely more than was conceivable. Professor S. N. Mukherjee's assessment of Sir William Jones's contribution to India may be taken as a definitive appreciation of the work of several generations of Indologists:

> ... India could hardly have withstood the cultural challenge of the west without drawing heavily on her past glory. It was Jones and his Society which he founded who discovered that India had produced a civilization equal to any other in the ancient world. The dignity and pride this discovery gave to the Indians is an undeniable factor in the growth of Indian nationalism.[6]

This enlightened facet of the colonial encounter stimulated, among a few Indian scholars and thinkers, an intellectual curiosity in their glorious past of high achievement, deemed legitimate areas of inquiry by European scholars. This energised a few Indians to seek a more authentic Hinduism, to purge it of some of its abominable excrescences. Among the Bengalis, with their own, supremely rich, literary heritage, their romance with music and poetry (the two are inseparable), and a more concentrated exposure to Western scholarship, in Calcutta, the impact was most comprehensive. Ram Mohan Roy (1772-1833), a Bengali Brahman who also read Persian, Hebrew, Greek, and English, was a visionary who embraced both the reinterpretation of Hinduism, which led him to the *Upanishads,* as well as social reform: the emancipation of women, the abolition of *sati* or the immolation of widows, the eradication of caste, and the necessity for legislation to initiate social reform (see Appendix II). (Indeed, K. M. Panikkar considers him 'the first feminist in India'). Ram Mohan Roy's *Brahmo Samaj* pioneered the reform of Hinduism. Although its success was not spectacular, it popularised a critical attitude to Hinduism and introduced the rudiments of a secular, analytic perspective. This was a principal pillar of the anti-colonial movement of the next century.[7]

It is incontrovertible that the spread of Western education, after 1835, and the work of the German-born, Oxford scholar, Friedrich Max Müller (1823-1900), a formidable authority in Sanskrit with an extraordinary empathy with the soul of ancient and modern India, deepened the critical strand in Indian thought and enlarged the heroic dimensions of the Aryan past. Max Müller's passionate enunciations, in England, on the source of the Aryan tradition and the character of its achievements, possibly more than any other factor, established an all-India pride in its Hindu antecedents.[8] This answered the void, the shame, fed by centuries of alien rule — Muslim, then British.

Max Müller argued that all Indo-European languages had a common origin; and that the ancient Aryans in India and their language, Sanskrit, were related to European peoples and their original languages, ancient Greek and Latin. Max Müller went further: he asserted that Indian and European peoples were descended from a common, ancient Aryan 'race'. Their ancestors were the South-Eastern and North-Western Aryans, respectively (see Appendix III). And in Ram Mohan Roy's visit to England (1831-1833; he died in Bristol on 27 September 1833), he discerned 'historical antecedents', culminating in 'the meeting again of the two great branches of the Aryan race'. In 1883, in an address in Bristol, to commemorate the 50th anniversary of Ram Mohan Roy's death, Max Müller said:

> In Rammohun [sic] Roy you may recognise the best representative of the South-Eastern Aryans, turning deliberately North, to shake hands once more with the most advanced outposts of the other branch of the Aryan family, established in these islands.
>
> .... long before his visit to England, England had visited India, first for the sake of commerce, then for the sake of self-defence and conquest. But for the sake of intellectual intercourse ... with his Aryan brothers, Rammohun Roy was the first who came from East to West, the first to join hands and complete that world-wide circle through which henceforth ... Oriental thought could run to the West, and Western thought return to the East, making us feel once more that ancient brotherhood which unites the whole Aryan race...[9]

Jawaharlal Nehru and Nirad Chaudhuri[10] have remarked on the profound impression which Max Müller's theories of Aryanism had on the shaping of a racial pride, a heroic self-image. Nehru, while conceding that Max Müller was 'carried away by his enthusiasm' in a Cambridge lecture of 1882, still quotes him with discernible pride, in self, and his Aryan progenitors. Max Müller had said:

> If I were asked under what sky the human mind has most fully developed some of its choicest gifts, has most deeply pondered on the greatest problems of life, and has found solutions to some of them which well deserve the attention even of those who have studied Plato and Kant — I should point to India. And if I were to ask myself from what literature we, here in Europe, who have been nurtured almost exclusively on the thoughts of Greeks and Romans, and of one Semitic race, the Jewish, may draw the corrective which is most

wanted in order to make our inner life more perfect, more comprehensive, more universal, in fact more truly human, a life, not for
this life only, but a transfigured and eternal life — again I should
point to India.[11]

Max Müller's celebration of the Aryan heritage of India fed a spate of
Aryanism, in India. This reached Indians overseas later; but it had similar
repercussions and the same promptings, as Tapan Raychaudhuri argues:
'A lack of cultural self-confidence, the continual need for assurance, prefer-
ably from reputable European quarters, was very much a part of the preoc-
cupation with the Hindu heritage... The belief that the white masters were
not very distant cousins of their brown Aryan subjects, provided a much-
needed salve to the wounded ego of the dependent elite'.[12]

Max Müller's influence on several major Hindu reformers was considerable. In the Punjab, Swami Dayananda (1824-1883), a Gujarati, founded
the *Arya Samaj* in 1875. He, like Ram Mohan Roy, advocated the cleansing
of contemporary Hinduism of its layers of superstition and other excrescences. Hinduism, he argued, had to return to its source, the *Vedas*,[13] the
original texts of the Aryans, which he deemed a divine revelation.[14] He considered caste, idolatry, Brahman privilege, and polytheism accretions,
with no foundation in the *Vedas:* these were the repository of all truth.[15] A
contemporary of Dayananda, a Bengali, Ramakrishna, also tried to cultivate the regeneration of Hinduism. But it was his erudite, articulate, flam-
boyant, western-educated disciple, Vivekananda (1863-1902), who made
a profound impression when he addressed the Parliament of Religions in
Chicago, in September 1893, who communicated, to the West, an ideal of
the richness of the spiritual inheritance of India; and the deep reservoir of
philosophical truths and intuitive living which the Indian tradition sustained. Vivekananda's acclamation in America assumed heroic dimensions
in India.[16] As Annie Besant, the radical Englishwoman from the
Theosophical Society, and one of the founders of the Benares Hindu University, observed of those momentous times: 'The Indian work is, first of

all, the revival, strengthening, and uplifting of the ancient religions. This act brought with it a new self-respect, a pride in the past, a belief in the future, and, and as an inevitable result, a great wave of patriotic life, the beginnings of the rebuilding of a nation'.[17] (Annie Besant had migrated to India in 1893, the year of Vivekananda's international acclaim).

India's renewal had found practical expression in the formation of the Indian National Congress, in December 1885. The new outlook, the Hindu reformation, was not narrowly chauvinistic, or slavishly atavistic. It blended a quest for roots, for intimations of ancient excellence, with an avid, unabashed pursuit of the humane, liberating treasures of the Western, liberal intellectual tradition. Nehru writes: 'While they drank from the rich streams of English literature, their minds were also full of ancient sages and heroes of India, their thoughts and deeds, and of the myths and traditions which they had imbibed from their childhood'.[18]

The late eminent Indian historian, Professor K. M. Panikkar, believes that the 'creation of a Hindu historiography and the recovery of India's great past constitute the most spectacular... the first fundamental contribution of European scholarship to India'. Recognition of the ancient achievements of the subject race, by the ruling race, gave to the former, possibilities of self-discovery, of renewal, of the will to give shape and meaning to the future. There were two sides to the colonial encounter: one which sprang from imperial greed, and was predicated on the certainty of European superiority and the barbarism of the 'native'; the other, often inspired by the loftiest of intellectual motives, applied the tools of European scholarship to discover, to give scholastic integrity, contextual rigour, to the frequently unrecorded and unassessed treasures of non-European achievements. India was a principal beneficiary of the latter.[19]

K. M. Panikkar considers Ram Mohan Roy the 'first modern man in India', profoundly shaped by early nineteenth century European liberalism. In Jawaharlal Nehru, the noble, universalistic strain in the English intellectual tradition — the pursuit of reason, the freedom to imagine, and the appreciation of beauty and excellence irrespective of its provenance — probably reached its apogee in India. And Nehru, in the mid-1930s, in the heat of the anti-colonial struggle, acknowledged his debt to England:

> Personally, I owe too much to England in my mental make-up ever to feel wholly alien to her. And, do what I will, I cannot get rid of the habits of mind, and the standards and ways of judging other countries, as well as life generally, which I acquired at school and college in England. My predilections (apart from the political ones) are in favour of England and the English people, and, if I have become what is called an uncompromising opponent of British rule in India, it is almost in spite of these.[20]

II

JOSEPH RUHOMON AND HIS 'DISCOVERY' OF INDIA, 1894

These intellectual promptings, also, were apprehended by one or two Indo-Guyanese men, in the 1890s. The long, often pedestrian, quest for self-expression, the longing to wipe out the dark image of the 'coolie', was the obsession of Joseph Ruhomon, almost certainly the first Indian intellectual in British Guiana. He was born in 1873 at Plantation Albion, Corentyne; his father, John Ruhomon, a chemist and druggist who had worked on several sugar plantations, was taken to British Guiana in 1859, aged eleven, along with his two brothers, aged thirteen and seven. They were not accompanied by their parents: the boys, apparently, were sight-seeing in Lucknow, United Provinces, when a recruiter persuaded them to go to Demerara (British Guiana).[21]

Joseph Ruhomon, though influenced profoundly by Christianity, showed an unquenchable curiosity in the literary riches of the Indian tradition, and the growing literature on Indian history and culture. He was literate in Hindi. Like his father, he was largely self-educated and, as his lectures in the 1920s and 1930s reveal, widely read in philosophy and history.[22] The writings of Professor Max Müller,who lifted Sanskrit literature to the scrutiny of European scholarship, fascinated him.[23]

Before Joseph Ruhomon, no Indian in British Guiana had tried to assess, critically, the condition of Indians 'at home and abroad'. Significantly, on 4

October 1894, a year after Vivekananda's magisterial oratorical expositions in Chicago, Ruhomon, aged twenty-one, presented an historic paper at St Leonard's Schoolroom in Georgetown. The text of this lecture was revised slightly and issued as a pamphlet soon afterwards, with an introduction by the Rev. H. V. P. Bronkhurst, Methodist Missionary to the Indians in British Guiana from 1861 to his death in 1895. *India: The Progress of Her People at Home and Abroad, and How Those in British Guiana may Improve Themselves* (Georgetown: C. K. Jardine,1894), was the first pamphlet by an Indian in the colony to be published.[24]

Joseph Ruhomon underlined his lineage with the great Indian tradition, delineated aspects of its high classical achievements, pointed to its substantial contemporary developments, and decried the social, cultural, and intellectual position of Indians in British Guiana. The latter notwithstanding, the young man was buoyed by what he had read of India's ancient heritage. Ruhomon spoke of pride in his race: 'East Indians [25] are an inherently great people and I feel supremely proud of the fact as one who has the pure, genuine East Indian blood flowing in his veins. In their own literature, science, and art, East Indians have held their own'. [26]

He quotes a contemporary, local source (possibly Bronkhurst) that India had produced poets, philosophers, and mathematicians, such as Vyas, Gautama, Kalidasa, Bhawanbhut, Aryabhat, Bhasker, Acharya, who ranked with the best of European thinkers. He countered the popular, but unexamined, view that India was devoid of the 'arts of civilised life', before the European encounter. Ruhomon argued that India was a prosperous, refined country, over three or four thousand years ago; and that the opulent range of beguiling 'masterpieces of art', which survives in contemporary India, could only have been crafted by 'minds refined and cultured'. He underlined this, adding that '... no one who has perused the pages of East Indian history... and studied the remains of ancient glory and of a departed greatness' could deny the ancient genius of 'my ancestral homeland... civilized, enlightened, India...' [27]

It is noteworthy that in the 1890s, Joseph Ruhomon's hometown, New

Amsterdam, had a small library, the Berbice Library. He was a member, and participated in the deliberations of its committee. The library carried a variety of 'colonial' and 'home' newspapers; and sponsored numerous lectures on a variety of subjects. The young Ruhomon, certainly, found himself in an environment which encouraged reading and discussion. During the last six months of 1893, when he was probably reading towards his 1894 lecture, the Berbice Library loaned 588 volumes; the highest number borrowed by one reader was twenty-one.[28] In early 1895, the secretary of the library reported: 'We need not again repeat what benefits the institution affords the community, and how pleased we are that so many continue to take advantage of these'.[29]

Ruhomon was 'discovering' India through European scholars; but the contemporary achievements of several Indians, in the West, and their recognition by the West, gave substance to his claims for, and celebration of, India's ancient past. This is how he described his enlightenment with regard to India; and the extent to which two contemporary events — the election of Dadabhai Naoroji (1825-1917) to the House of Commons in 1892; and Vivekananda's magisterial oratorical feats, in Chicago, in September 1893 — lifted him. He recalled proudly:

> Not a very long time ago... I was utterly insensible to the real progress of my race in India... But I accidentally had a plunge into East Indian Literature, — books, magazines... devoted to the interests of my race... I saw that India could boast of great men and great women — great thinkers and great writers — as great as any that Europe or any other country has produced — poets, philosophers, scientists, and so on...[30]

Ruhomon was especially proud of Naoroji, the first Indian M. P. in the Commons, noting that 'Mr. Naoroji speaks with an authority on Indian matters which certainly no one else can claim...' [31] He believed that Naoroji's achievements conferred dignity and honour on all Indians and that this was not lost on them, for in January 1894, when Naoroji visited India, the people accorded him a welcome which 'probably transcended anything that India had ever granted to any man since she came under the rule of Great Britain'. Ruhomon exhorted his Indo-Guyanese compatriots to take pride in the attainments of the 'grand distinguished East Indian in England, the "Grand Old Man of India" ':

> Our earnest prayers as East Indians should be that not only may this good man long live to be an honour to his race and country, but that God may raise up other Naorojis who shall be instrumental in furthering the interests of, and pouring down streams of blessing upon, our glorious Fatherland.[32]

The impact of Vivekananda's expositions in Chicago in 1893, his oratorical exhibition of compelling lucidity, depth, and magnanimity of spirit, enthralled America. Vivekananda, aged thirty, responded keenly to the dominant theme, the central prompting, of tolerance and the softening of dogmatic certainties, at the Parliament of Religions. As Romain Rolland, the French writer who communed with the soul of modern India, wrote: 'Each of the orators had spoken of his God, of the God of his sect. He (Vivekananda) — he alone — spoke of all their Gods, and embraced them all in the Universal Being'.[33]

The enthusiastic response of *The New York Herald* to Vivekananda must have struck a chord with Indians such as Joseph Ruhomon, who had converted to Christianity and, privately, probably agonised over the interminable calumny heaped on their ancestral religion: 'Undoubtedly the greatest figure in the Parliament of Religions. After hearing him we feel how foolish it is to send missionaries to this learned nation'.[34] Romain Rolland wrote that Vivekananda's speech in Chicago was 'like a tongue of flame. Among the grey wastes of cold dissertation, it fired the souls of the listening throng'.[35] Joseph Ruhomon, speaking a year after Vivekananda's mesmeric performances in September 1893, saw them as an Indian achievement:

... my soul was thrilled through and through with genuine pleasure and admiration when I learnt that there were many brilliant East Indian lights in the world of English oratory; who were Burkes and Pitts, and Gladstones, and Talmages, in the glorious Anglo-Saxon tongue — a striking instance of which was afforded us when at the Great World's Parliament of religions held in Chicago a few months ago, some of our East Indian orators who stood up on the platform as champions of their own religions, simply electrified the vast audience by their marvellous exhibitions in English oratory.[36]

Ruhomon was a Christian; but his 'discovery' of India, the pre-Moghul, pre-Muslim India — ancient Hindu India of high artistic and diverse, pioneering, secular excellence, appealed to a deeper, more elemental, racial yearning. Like most Indian thinkers at the end of the last century, he knew that the ancient Indian achievement had been initially unearthed, recognised, and given intellectual solidity by European scholarship. This bred a reverence for the western, liberal tradition, but the knowledge that the achievement was Indian also fed a spirit of self-confidence, an optimism for the regeneration of India, and a notion of illimitable possibilities for an indigenous Indian contribution. Ruhomon observed confidently:

Our people have been great in the past, and they will be greater yet in the future. The signs of the times point to the brilliant future of the East Indian race....[37] we know there is a golden harvest to be reaped by East Indians... In their own country native Indians have proved themselves to be qualified to hold positions that are held by Europeans. As doctors, ministers, legal practitioners, politicians, authors, editors of newspapers, etc., they are certainly not inferior in ability to Europeans. On the contrary, they have proved themselves to be equal in ability, if not superior, to their fair-faced brothers. They have, indeed, drunk deep draughts at the fountain of European thought and learning, and there is no question about their being beaten in competition with Europeans. The time is fast coming when the Indians will be able to live independently of British rule, will have the powers of Government thrust into their own hands, and will know how to look after their own affairs and take care of themselves.[38]

From this vantage point of immense self-assurance, he surveyed the condition of his compatriots in British Guiana. He lamented the intellectual and social void within the Indian community; and contrasted this with what he considered the superior mental, moral, religious, and social accomplishments of the Black and Coloured peoples. He remarked on the growing tendency for the latter to provide higher education for their children — secondary, as well as professional, education, in Britain. Ruhomon attributed this to their deeper social consciousness, nurtured by a variety of social and religious organisations.[39]

Ruhomon's verdict on his people's record in British Guiana up to the early 1890s, is rather dark, and somewhat inaccurate: 'We have done nothing in the Colony that has redounded to our credit...[40] The great majority of our people are weak and ignorant... The East Indian race in British Guiana has not yet begun its history as a race. Its past has been chaos and darkness'.[41] However, this harsh,self-deprecating tenor must be seen as the impetuous lamentations of an impatient native son, anxious to accelerate the pace of change, to reach the heights attained by some of his compatriots elsewhere; to erase the 'coolie' shame.

It is necessary to note that in the early 1890s, the rice and cattle industries in British Guiana were in their embryonic stage; Indian people's energies were directed to the acquisition of land; they tended to view western, denominational education as subversive of their ethos. But something *was* being achieved: Tyran Ramnarine argues, persuasively, that the early generations of Indians concentrated on establishing a 'sound economic base which laid the foundation for the next generation's mobility aspirations'.[42]

Ruhomon regretted that there were no Indian doctors or lawyers, no

Indian legislators, no organisations to foster the social and intellectual uplift of his people. And echoing Vivekananda's extolling of *abhay,* fearlessness and strength, he exhorted Indo-Guyanese to be fearless, to be strong:

> ....it is high time now that they awake to their own interest, and put forth their best efforts towards improving themselves in this Colony. Our people must be bold, strong, fearless, acquitting themselves like men. Never be afraid... of the derisive criticism of your enemies, or the sneers and scoffs of pessimists, and the many barriers which may stand in your pathway...[44]

Ruhomon did not despair. He implored Indians to educate their sons *and* daughters; and he challenged the young men and young women to cultivate their intellect. He believed that women were 'one of the most powerful forces at work in this 19th century, not only for the emancipation of her sex, but in the common cause of humanity'; and that Indians in British Guiana would gain infinitely more if men *and* women worked together, in 'the noble object of promoting the interests of our race...' [45]He argued that it was crucial to form organisations in order to advance the aspirations of the community, and that such organisations should publish regular newspapers as a means of educating and informing the wider community.[46] He also advocated the building of a library. An omnivorous reader of good books, the young Ruhomon explained:

> Books are one of the greatest blessings in life, and the educated mind which dives into literature, enjoys a pleasure of which the rude uncultured mind knows nothing... You have the glorious gift of intellect — cultivate it by the numerous means which are at your disposal, and you shall enjoy a pleasure that is genuine and lasting and true. [47]

He lamented the early death of the British Guiana East Indian Institute (founded in 1892), almost certainly the first, secular Indian organisation started by Indians in the Caribbean. Its principal architects were Thomas Flood, Veerasawmy Mudaliar,[48] James Wharton, and his brother, William Hewley Wharton. The 'founder' was William Hewley Wharton; James Wharton was the secretary. The Institute sent an illuminated congratulatory address to Dadabhai Naoroji, the first Indian M.P. in Britain, who won the seat of Finsbury Central by three votes in July 1892 (see Appendix V).[49] The brevity of the Institute's existence has been attributed to the atmosphere of indifference to intellectual and political pursuits prevalent among Indo-Guyanese in the 1890s [50], in conjunction with the historic departure of William Hewley Wharton for Edinburgh University, in 1893. Wharton, the son of Hindu indentured labourers, was born on 20 August 1869. He was probably the first Indian in the Caribbean to study at a British university. He graduated as a doctor of medicine, at Edinburgh, in 1899.[51]

Throughout his university years (1893-1899), he was identified closely with Indian affairs; and in 1896, was elected secretary of the Edinburgh Indian Association. (This had been founded in 1883 to meet the social and cultural needs of Indian students at Edinburgh. In that year, it comprised a mere six Indian students; by 1900, its membership included 200 Indian students and several Scottish supporters).[52] Wharton was instrumental in promoting a concert which yielded £200 for famine relief to India, in 1896. In 1898-1899, he was elected president of the Association. He was proud to be identified with the land of his parents and recorded, with evident delight, the high commendation accorded him by Professor Sir Thomas Grainger Stewart, Physician-in-Ordinary to Queen Victoria, on 7 January 1899. The occasion was the annual dinner of the Edinburgh Indian Association. In his toast to the Association, Professor Stewart remarked of Wharton:

Here is a young gentleman who was born in British Guiana, possesses an English name, fills the chair at this banquet with much dignity and grace, and still insists in calling himself an Indian. I may as well call myself an Indian, as we both belong to the same common stock

— the Aryan family.[53]

On 24 June 1899, at an Edinburgh Indian Association debate, Wharton successfully defended the proposition: 'That the further social emancipation of Indian women is desirable'. It is noteworthy that Wharton and Ruhomon were Christians; but their discovery of the rich heritage of Aryan India, and the linking of that inheritance to Europe, however remotely, by Professor Max Müller, imbued them with a profound sense of their own self-worth.

Max Müller's influence ran deep: he corresponded with Prime Minister Gladstone; Queen Victoria knew him personally and was familiar with his notion of Aryanism. Indeed, as early as January 1863, he had lectured in comparative philology to the Royal family, on the Isle of Wight. Queen Victoria was present; and Max Müller reported to his wife: 'She (the Queen) listened very attentively, and did not knit at all, though her work was brought in'. The Queen's private secretary later informed Müller that she was very pleased with the lectures.[54] Is it surprising, then, that in India, by the late nineteenth century, Max Müller was 'a legend and an institution'? [55]

So, although Joseph Ruhomon was pained by what he saw as the pedestrian progress of his compatriots in British Guiana, he had hope because ancient India and the Aryan tradition, with its high intellectual pedigree, were his. Not only had his ancestors achieved greatness, but through the Aryan connection, they and the current rulers of India were racially linked. This, in an environment where everyone tended to look down upon the 'coolie', had vast powers of redemption. Ruhomon celebrated his Aryan roots in his lecture of 4 October 1894:

> Today I am not only convinced, as I am sure all of you in this room tonight are, of the greatness of India as a country, and the greatness of her sons and daughters as a people, but I am joyfully and confidently anticipating the time when in intelligence, in culture, in morals

and intellectual attainments, the great East Indian Race [sic] shall be second to none in the world... I may add... that we also in British Guiana with all our ancestors in India are closely allied by blood relationship to the British nation, as the following poem by Ben Elvry entitled 'To India'.. will show:-

'Brave brothers, of the sun-kissed face
Heirs of the ancient Arya name;
Like heritage with you we claim,
Our tongue betrays our kindred race...[56]

However, this neither changed the actual position of Indians in British Guiana nor the way they were regarded. In September 1892, for example, *The Daily Chronicle*, in a leader on the Report of the Immigration Agent General for 1891, noted that Indians in British Guiana served 'the purpose for which they are imported to the colony very admirably indeed'; adding that they were 'the very breath in the industrial nostrils of its... existence'. However, the paper regretted that the people whose achievements were documented in the Report, 'evince not the slightest interest in regard thereto'.[57] In September 1891, *The Argosy* applauded the 'unostentatious manner' in which D. W. D. Comins, the delegate from India, investigated 'the condition of the coolies' surroundings on sugar estates', 'the homes of the coolies', etc. This, it concluded, gave 'the coolies no direct inducement to suppose that he [Comins] had come here to enquire into charges laid or suspicions entertained, by the authorities he represented, against the coolies' employers'.[58]

It was this lowly image of the Indian in the colony — the menial, ignorant 'coolie' — which gnawed at the dignity of educated Indians, an experience shared by the educated elite in India as well. The 'discovery' of ancient India with its pioneering accomplishments in many areas of high culture — initially, almost wholly the work of European scholars such as Jones and his colleagues in the Asiatic Society of Bengal — gave to Ram

Mohan Roy, Swami Dayananda, Vivekananda, Rabindranath Tagore, Jawaharlal Nehru, Joseph Ruhomon, and William Hewley Wharton that essential redefinition of self, which enabled them, in their individual ways, to challenge imperial definitions; indeed, to begin to undermine imperial supremacy.

Nirad Chaudhuri, the biographer of Professor Max Müller, has given us a touching comment on this great Anglo-German scholar's vital role in India's renewal. Max Müller's work encapsulates the many enduring, positive legacies of the Indo-European encounter. Chaudhuri explains: 'The human urge in all his scholarly work was that, becoming aware of their great past and drawing on their legacy, they would revitalise their contemporary life, and shed the dead wood which had accumulated through the centuries'.[59] In British Guiana, in the 1890s, Ruhomon and Wharton were among the first beneficiaries of this legacy.

III

INDIA'S WAR EFFORT AND INDO-GUYANESE LOYALTY TO THE EMPIRE, 1914-1918

... the British Empire is sustained by the studied policy of eminent states-men on broad principles of tolerance and justice and not bigotry and fanati-cism ... Indians claim... their religious rights on the Magna Carta of that illustrious British Queen Victoria of revered memory.
Ayube M. Edun (Secretary, British Guiana East Indian Association), Letter to the Editor, *The Daily Argosy*, 28 July 1926

Admiration for India and a reverence for ancient Indian values, did not conflict with Indo-Guyanese loyalty to the British Empire. Indeed, it could be argued that the sumptuous regal embroidery of the Empire, with Queen Victoria (the Empress of India), in particular, acquiring a halo of divinity, had intimations of the ethereal dimensions of *Rama Raj*, the Golden Age of Lord Rama, in the *Ramayana*. It is fascinating that this hitherto inarticulate Indian community in British Guiana, could muster the enthusiasm and energy to send 'illuminated' addresses to Queen Victoria, on her diamond jubilee, in 1897, [60] and to King George V, on his accession in 1911 [61] (see Appendix VI). This initiative probably sprang from the reverence for the regal persona in classical Hinduism. One reads in the *Ramayana:*

Where the land is kingless the cloud, lightning-wreathed and loud-voiced, gives no rain to the earth.

Where the land is kingless the son does not honour his father, nor the wife her husband.

Where the land is kingless men do not meet in assemblies, nor make lovely gardens and temples.

Where the land is kingless the rich are unprotected, and shepherds and peasants sleep with bolted doors.

A river without water, a forest without grass, a herd of cattle without a herdsman, is the land without a king.[62]

The attribution of virtual divinity to Queen Victoria, for instance, is adumbrated in Joseph Ruhomon's poem, 'Threnody', a lamentation on the death of the Queen, in January 1901:

> ... no more will our lov'd Queen, with heart truly royal,
>   stand by our side!
> Darksome the Throne lies — robbed of Her Presence
>   sublime that made it the pride
> And glory of Britain — the envy of nations on earth
>   far and wide.
>
> Snapped by the death-blow is the cord of Her great
>   love that round us she twined.
> No more will she guide us onwards and upward with
>   Her strong soul and mind,
> So amply enlightened with wisdom divine for the good
>   of mankind...

Victoria! Thy name long for ages shall live in song
   and in story,
Still cheering, still guiding the Empire on with the
   light of its glory —
Aye, still moving the hearts of its rulers to act
   wisely and nobly.[63]

Before 1916, no Indo-Guyanese had been elected to the legislature; and colonial administrators frequently decried their apathy in exercising the franchise, or contesting the general elections. However, these authorities reacted with typical imperial arrogance and paranoia, whenever educated, articulate men from India visited the colony. Pandit Parmanand Saraswat, a distinguished *Arya Samaj* missionary from the Punjab, arrived in British Guiana on 28 December 1910. The Government refused to allow him to deliver a lecture at the Immigration Department. He subsequently gave his lecture, 'Ancient India', at the Town Hall, Georgetown (see Appendix VII). The problem was that the Government of India deemed him 'a dangerous man', and had requested information on his activities overseas, including British Guiana. Pandit Parmanand's crime was that he was articulating pride in an ancient, pre-Muslim, Hindu India; engendering a resurgence of Indian self-respect and self-confidence, rooted in an Aryan atavism; thus cultivating notion of the Indians' capacity to govern themselves.

Later, Governor Hodgson sought special legislation to deport Dr Ram Narain Sharma, another Indian national, who was living in the colony. However, the Government of India did not support his deportation: they argued that this would be construed in India as a discriminatory act against Indians in British Guiana. In 1916, the surveillance of Sharma and censorship of his mail were increased; he was 'under suspicion in connection with the propagation of sedition amongst East Indians in the colony, with certain classes of whom he appears to have influence'. Meanwhile, the Government of British Guiana, especially during World War 1, seized Indian nationalist newspapers originating overseas and addressed to local subscribers: *The Free Hindustan, India, Ghadr,* and *Bande Mataram* were deemed to have a 'mischievous effect'.[64]

Such repressive imperial censorship, inevitably, bred an irrepressible curiosity among Indo-Guyanese, in the 'Motherland', India. This resurgent patriotism, however, was not incompatible with continual expressions of loyalty to the King and the Empire. The latter were perceived as virtually sacrosanct, transcending the pettiness and meanness of 'the man on the spot'. Indo-Guyanese conceptions of the Empire, it would seem, were closely identified with the person of the Sovereign, the Empress or Emperor of India.

Thus, when in August 1916, a broad cross-section of Guyanese leaders — Blacks, Coloureds, Portuguese — were demanding the recall of the Governor, Sir Walter Egerton, prominent Indians categorically dissociated themselves from the recall movement. At a meeting in Georgetown on 28 August, they pledged their loyalty to the Empire:

> As loyal East Indians we feel that when the Empire of which we have the honour to belong, is in the throes of the greatest war the world has ever known, petty dissension and personal spite should be subservient to that spirit of unity and patriotism which has ever characterised the British colonies, when the Mother Country [Britain] has been threatened with danger.[65]

The prominent Indian businessman, Thomas Flood, who chaired the meeting, explained that in reaffirming their loyalty to the Empire, 'We are only following the footsteps of our noble India... she showed her loyalty by sending to Great Britain her best men and treasures, and will do so until the end'.[66]

Indeed, the Indian National Congress, in December 1914, had pledged its 'profound devotion to the Throne', and its 'unswerving allegiance to the British connection'.[67] On 1 January 1916, *The Daily Argosy* of British Guiana reported that 'millions in India [were] waiting to serve'. It added that the presidential address at the annual session of the Indian National Congress was permeated by unbridled loyalty to the Empire, and pride in India's contribution to the war effort: '...the supreme feeling was one of admiration of Britain bearing the burden in the struggle for liberty, and a pride in India having proved herself abreast of the rest of the Empire in assistance to the Mother country, the spontaneous outburst of loyalty dispelling forever all distrust between Indians and their rulers'.

India's material support was equally solid. By 1918, India had sent 1,302,394 soldiers to the War — these constituted the largest force from any country in the Empire, after Britain. She also contributed skilled personnel: 1,069 officers of the medical service, 360 officers of the Army Medical Corps, 1,200 nursing sisters, 2,142 assistant and sub-assistant surgeons. About 100,000 Indians were killed in battle. India sent 172,815 animals, and 3,691,836 tons of supplies. Her annual contribution of between £20,000,000 and £30,000,000, during the War, was an astounding effort: her central revenues were less than £100,000,000 per year. Moreover, India gave £100,000,000 to the British Government, towards the end of the War.[68]

It is noteworthy that the Indians were told repeatedly that the War was absolutely necessary to stem the tide of German barbarism: the British fed notions of high moral imperatives. India's impressive war effort bred a recognition, among Indians, that they deserved a better deal in the Empire: they would not tolerate barbarism at home.

In British Guiana, also, the 'Hun' was indicted for 'senseless crimes against civilisation and humanity'; whereas the Empire was seen as prosecuting the war in 'the noblest English traditions...cleanly, against a ruthless and conscienceless foe'. [69] Joseph Ruhomon mirrored the lofty, somewhat idyllic, expectations of many Indo-Guyanese, at the end of the War. In a poem, redolent of allusions to *Rama Raj*, 'The Golden Age', he dreamt, in December 1918, of the reign of 'Faith and Honour, Justice and Freedom...the great ideals set by the nations who have stood against the Antichrist...':

Yes, a Golden Age is surely dawning for the tortured
Race of Man. Old things have passed away for
Ever in the purging flames of war, and
A newer order cometh, a new race,
Reborn, regenerated, with nobler
Aims and more exalted purpose... [70]

Yet, on 13 April 1919, British troops massacred unarmed Indians at
Amritsar, in the Punjab: 379 were killed; 1,200 wounded. Percival Spear
argues that after Amritsar, 'a scar was drawn across Indo-British relations
deeper than any which had been inflicted since the Mutiny'.[71] Gandhi called
Amritsar 'a wanton cruelty and inhumanity, almost unparalleled in modern
times' [72]: barbarism had survived the defeat of the 'Hun', he seemed to be
saying.

The expectations of reform engendered by India's war effort, and the
precipitate, violent abrogation of hope at Amritsar, so soon after the War,
were a powerful catalyst for the militant expression of Indian nationalism.
The Indians in British Guiana saw the struggle in India as their own; and
were inspired to claim their own rights because of the high, almost divine,
moral tone which Gandhi's leadership, in the 1920s, conferred on the
Indian National Congress.

Thus, in February 1920, when the British Guiana East Indian Association (BGEIA) opposed the Seditious Publications Bill, which they considered an instrument of thought-control, they deemed it 'a grave indictment
on their loyalty and patriotism' [73] — precisely the soil in which nationalist
protest in India, after the War, was rooted. It is also interesting that Francis
Kawall of the BGEIA labelled the Bill 'a reverse of civilisation' [74] — a subtle
allusion to the ethos which supposedly informed the War effort. The Bill
was 'indefinitely postponed'. [75]

From the 1920s, Indo-Guyanese loyalty to the Empire was refracted,
increasingly, through a deep, rich identity with the cultural treasures of
ancient India, and a new, Gandhian India, which was perceived as spiritu-

ally, morally strong. This had special resonances for Indians in British Guiana, after 1920. The old badge of shame — indentureship — was abolished on 16 April 1920. But impressive progress with rice and cattle, and the establishment of an Indian middle class based on shop-keeping and the professions, co-existed with considerable illiteracy: the 'coolie' shadow lingered. Pride in a new, rising India, answered the yearning for ancestral greatness, spawned by Indo-Guyanese material achievements after the War; but this, as noted earlier, did not vitiate their loyalty to the Empire.

Nothing encapsulated this duality better than the button issued by the British Guiana East Indian Association in 1920. The Association announced that it would be an inch in diameter, bordered with red, white and blue. The release continued:

> The words 'B.G.E.I.A.' will be printed inside the circle, with the date of the founding of the Association, 22/4/19. In the centre of the button will be a miniature map of India on Mercator's projection, this being fitted into a shield on the top of which is the national flag of India. Immediately under the shield is the motto, in Hindi character: 'Unity is strength'.[76]

Throughout the 1920s, one discerns a more comprehensive loyalty and reverence for India; and that a sense of belonging to British Guiana and the Empire, though expanding, was mediated by resurgent pride in India. This was what permeated the inaugural address by J. A. Luckhoo, the first Indo-Guyanese legislator, to the resuscitated BGEIA, on 24 April 1919, in Georgetown:

> As a community we feel we have reached the turn of the tide not only in our life in the colony but in the history of our race and country. India has played a worthy part in the great conflict of nations, and has helped in no small measure to roll back the tide of anarchy and barbarism that was threatening to engulf the world.

By virtue of her loyalty to the throne, in its hour of greatest peril, she has been admitted to the Councils of the Empire... India can now look forward to a greater measure of self-government and greater freedom in determining her own affairs.

We, in British Guiana, feel it incumbent on us to rise to the occasion and make ourselves worthy of the great race to which we belong.

We feel the time has arrived when we must collect our forces together, in one grand effort, to achieve the high and noble destiny to which we feel we are now called. [77]

IV

GANDHI AND INDO-GUYANESE PRIDE IN THE 'MOTHERLAND' IN THE 1920s

In Trinidad as well, by 1920, Indian nationalism had captured the imagination of the local Indians. *The East Indian Herald* carried an article, 'The Lessons of the I.N.C.', which was reproduced in *The Daily Argosy* (British Guiana), on 2 April 1920. It exhorted Indians in the West Indies to identify with the Indian nationalist struggle, and to uphold the traditions of the 'Motherland':

> Today our kinsmen in the Motherland (India) are constitutionally fighting for self-government; a government on the same basis as that enjoyed by the other self-governing dominions within the Empire. It behoves us, as sons of India, to do all we can to help them in their momentous struggle. It is our duty to make our brethren at home feel that we who have migrated, are not a distinct loss to the Motherland, but a great asset for a growing Indian nation.

Gandhi and the Indian National Congress received copious coverage in the newspapers in British Guiana. Editorial comments appeared frequently, on various aspects of the nationalist movement and their implications for the Empire, as well as Indians in British Guiana. *The Daily Argosy,* however, took a fiercely imperialistic line on Indian issues. Its editor, Samuel Lupton, was infamous for his intransigence, his raucous, jingoistic denigration of Gandhi: he could see nothing but subversion behind the nationalist cause. An Englishman, who, for some years, had edited a newspaper in Karachi, Lupton regularly expressed the bigotry and racial arrogance characteristic of many Anglo-Indians. But, unwittingly, he contributed immeasurably to the virtual deification of Gandhi, among Indo-Guyanese. Framed pictures of the Mahatma achieved a place of divine eminence amidst those of Hindu deities, in their homes, whatever their social status.

Meanwhile, the prominence given, in the 1920s, to the Colonisation Scheme — an abortive plan to devise a new system of immigration from India — meant that links with India were not abruptly severed with the end of indentureship. Several Indian delegates visited the colony: Pillai and Tivary in 1922, Kunwar Maharaj Singh in 1925, and the Rev. C. F. Andrews in 1929.[78] The spirit of revolt in India, following the Amritsar massacre in April 1919, was transmitted, in subtle ways, by these visitors from the 'Motherland', as well as by J. A. Luckhoo and Dr. William Hewley Wharton, who spent several months in India in 1919-1920 and 1924, primarily to persuade Gandhi that the renewal of Indian immigration was in the interest of India and Indo-Guyanese. Luckhoo and Wharton met Gandhi, Motilal Nehru, and many other leaders of Indian opinion; but the climate in India, after Amritsar, was not conducive to Indian immigration. However, Luckhoo was driven by the idea that an Indian Colony could be established in British Guiana, if more Indians could be brought into the colony.[79]

In an extraordinary intervention, at a meeting of the British Guiana Colonisation Deputation with Lord Sinha, the Under-Secretary of State at the India Office, in London, on 7 August 1919, J. A. Luckhoo pleaded:

> ...in British Guiana, although we form 40 per cent of the population, we feel and we have always felt that we are scattered sons of India, and that India should stretch her hands across to us and try and help us and lift us up. The only way of doing this is to increase our numbers in the colony... we hope that in the future British Guiana will

become a great Indian Colony. We appeal to the Head of the India Office, and to the leaders of Indian authority and opinion to give us their help. We feel that you have our destiny in your hands, and we ask you to remember that these people who emigrate to British Guiana will have the same rights, and that if they will come in sufficient numbers, we shall be able to build up an Indian Colony which will be a credit to India and the Empire.[80]

Nothing came of this grandiose idea; but it was a barometer of the rising Indian self-confidence in British Guiana,[81] and the impact of the idealism of Gandhi. Moreover, Lupton's denunciation of Gandhi hastened the Mahatma's ascendancy to virtual sainthood in the colony. In December 1920, *The Daily Argosy* called Gandhi an 'unbalanced fanatic', who had done much 'mischief' because of his non-co-operation programme. But it conceded that many Indians in British Guiana acknowledged Gandhi as 'their political leader'. [82] In January 1921, the paper denounced Gandhi and 'the extremists' for their opposition to the Colonisation Scheme, and lamented their 'seditious agitation' and its potential consequences for the integrity of the Empire, at a time when the Bolsheviks were advancing southwards and eastwards in Asia. The paper argued:

If the extremist section of Indian opinion is allowed to work its will, the gate will have been opened for similar excesses in Egypt, South Africa, and other colonies. The effect of this will be felt throughout the Empire, and not the least, in the colony in which we live.[83]

In March 1922, *The Daily Argosy* reported that 'India's non-co-operationist leader', Gandhi, was arrested and charged with sedition.[84] In a leader, in July 1923, it deplored the circulation, in the colony, of propaganda material of the 'political extremists in India', contending that this exercise was designed to raise funds for the 'agitation in India against the British Raj'. *The Argosy* hoped that Indo-Guyanese would spurn such efforts, as they could have little sympathy for the cause of the 'extremists'. The paper concluded, somewhat despairingly:

> In all the publications, as also in articles published in local newspapers, great play is made with the name of Mr. Gandhi, and so far as we can judge, local East Indians regard that ascetic and firebrand as a kind of minor deity...[85]

The liberal *Daily Chronicle*, however, (under the editorship of A.R.F. Webber in the early 1920s), came closer to Indian opinion in British Guiana, when it noted, perceptively, that it was not Gandhi who was undermining the British Empire, but men like General Dyer, the 'infamous butcher' of Amritsar, who treated 'educated Indians, men of refinement and culture, as though they were helots and underdogs'. The paper argued that the incarceration of Gandhi, even his banishment, would make no difference: 'The spirit of India is awake; and it will be met, not by the methods of General Dyer... but by wise and courageous statesmanship'.[86]

But Lupton's *Daily Argosy* was unrepentant, unremitting in its vilification of Gandhi. In February 1925, it carried a caption: GANDHI A HERETIC — ATTACK ON HINDU RELIGION. A scurrilous piece followed, inspired by a report from India that Hindu leaders in Bombay had repudiated Gandhi's assertion that he was dedicated to the abolition of untouchability. Lupton mischievously concluded that the latter commitment was subversive of Hinduism, therefore, Gandhi was a heretic [87] — a lame attempt to diminish his Himalayan stature.

In March 1925, Alfred Ramsing (sic), an Indo-Guyanese from Georgetown, reproached Lupton for underrating the 'intellectual powers' of the people of India, in his editorial comment that Indians were incapable of governing themselves. Ramsing countered that there were Indian men who could 'give lessons on the science of government (*rajniti*)'; and with subtle sagacity, he indicted the Raj: 'The first rudiment on the science of government is to govern with justice and humanity; and if the English people will learn to exercise these two essential qualities to a better degree, or consistently with the principles of Christianity, they will have compassed the whole range of this great science'.

Lupton was implacable. He replied immediately, with undiminished racial arrogance:

> It is a great undertaking to govern 320,000,000 people, and for the British Raj to abandon it task and hand over the reins of government to a small political party [the Indian National Congress] which does not contain a single man of first-class intellect, but is chiefly composed of unsuccessful lawyers and semi-educated persons who have failed to secure on their merits even minor posts under the British administration, none of whom have any practical experience of administration, would be inflicting a terrible punishment upon the great and helpless mass of the people of India.[88]

The Argosy also reserved some venom for Indian 'agitators' in British Guiana; it even tried to to sow dissension among local Indians. Commenting on the outbreak of Hindu-Muslim riots in India, in June 1926, it asserted that the demands for self-government by the 'extremist Swarajists' looked absurd in light of these 'ugly realities'. Lupton asked, sarcastically, alluding to J. A. Luckhoo's call for an Indian Colony in British Guiana: 'Is this state of affairs... one of the blessings in store for British Guiana when the Indian agitators in our midst have succeeded in their resolve to make it an 'Indian Colony'?...'[89]

However, Hindu - Muslim unity in British Guiana was more robust than anywhere in the Indian diaspora, including neighbouring Trinidad. In 1929, C. F. Andrews acknowledged the presence of religious tolerance, and applauded the erosion of the stigma of caste among Indo-Guyanese. In a lecture delivered, appropriately enough, at the East Indian Cricket Club — an enduring symbol of Indian unity in the colony — Andrews expressed satisfaction that they had 'completely obliterated' the deep-seated religious barrier between Hindus and Muslims. He observed that Hindu, Muslim, and Christian Indians sat at the same table, and shared the same meal. Moreover, he never saw the stubborn signs of religious conflict that were prevalent in India; nor did he encounter the 'great gulf of social distinction', rooted in caste.[90]

Even Lupton was able to recognise this commendable achievement by Indians in British Guiana: Hindu-Muslim unity. He wrote, in March 1929, that 'they have... succeeded in conquering the intense hostility between Hindu and Muslim which has figured so largely in Indian history, and which breaks out periodically even today, in spite of the restraining and pacificatory influence of the British Raj...'[91]

The progressive editor, A. R. F. Webber, always empathised with the pursuit of cultural dignity and economic security by Indo-Guyanese. He was an astute interpreter of the momentous events in India, and a sympathetic chronicler of changing attitudes among Indo-Guyanese. In July 1927, he wrote: 'The days of foreign rule in Eastern lands are numbered. Imperialism has been weighed in the balance and found wanting. Only time is needed to seal its doom...'[92] At this time, the British Guiana East Indian Association was a vigorous campaigner against the Colonial Office's resolute commitment to replace the colony's representative constitution, which was elective but severely limited in franchise, with Crown Colony Government. Webber acknowledged this, and added:

> ...the East Indian are, if anything, more valiant in the fight than the Negro element. They have imbibed the spirit of the struggle in India. They know only too well what Crown Colony Government has meant in India, and they are determined to resist to the last breath of man and horse.[93]

Gandhi epitomised that contagious 'spirit of struggle' in the 'motherland': Indo-Guyanese virtually enthroned him in their pantheon of Gods.

V

INDIAN CULTURAL RESURGENCE IN BRITISH GUIANA —
THE 1920s

It was primarily at the cultural and religious levels that the Indian nationalist movement inspired a resurgence in the colony. The enthusiastic response of educated, Christian Indians, before the First World War, to the 'discovery' of India, has already been discussed. This found organisational expression in the 1920s. The work of the small [Wesleyan] East Indian Young Men's Society, in which Peter Ruhomon (the brother of Joseph Ruhomon) was a principal force, reflected the fascination which India exerted on young, educated Indo-Guyanese.[94]

In October 1919, at the inaugural meeting of the Society, the acting Governor of British Guiana, Cecil Clementi (1875-1947), gave a lecture on 'The Kinship of the Indian and British Peoples'. Arguing on the basis of Max Müller's philological premises, he asserted: 'The ethnical conclusion is that the inhabitants of the British Isles and India are of the same origin, far off it is true, but nevertheless real'.[95] Clementi was an erudite man, a respected classical scholar. His linking of Aryan India to Europe, as Joseph Ruhomon had done in 1894, must have provided a powerful, initial boost to his young listeners' self-image — no longer mere 'coolie' boys. Thus while Lupton, the editor of *The Daily Argosy,* was decrying Gandhi and the 'extremists' in India, the East Indian Young Men's Society cultivated and deepened its focus on India and the ancient Indian heritage.[96]

In March 1922, for example, Rev. Stanley Edwards, who had spent a year in Calcutta, delivered a lecture, 'Impressions of India', to the Society. The exquisite, supremely rich architecture of Indian temples and palaces evoked in him a sense of wonder. He explained: 'A great many things have the impress of time, a sense of antiquity... To look upon these one felt one was in the presence of a people truly great'. Rev. Edwards confided that he could 'bow down in reverence' to the people who had created such stupendous works of art, beguiling feats of the imagination — achievements which could humble Western minds. His observations on the future of India, too, would have lifted his young Indo-Guyanese audience, feeding their new, brighter sense of self-worth, while sharpening their curiosity in their ancestral land:

> I believe there is moving among the young men of India a magnificent spirit which is going to be, in its own way, something of the spirit of the Crusaders. They are working for the deliverance of their country from the ills and evils which grind men in the dust... When it comes into its own, India would be in the van of the great nations of the world, and will make a noble contribution to the welfare of the whole of humanity.[97]

Another organisation, the Christian Indian Society, was formed in early 1923. At its inaugural meeting, Rev. James Persaud, an Indo-Guyanese Anglican minister, lectured on 'Vedic India'. His presentation was summarised thus: '... [he] dealt with the subject from the Aryan invasion, prior to which, he said, little is known of India. After dealing with the ethnological and philological aspects of the subject, he rapidly traversed the high civilisation attained by India in the remote past, in relation to art, science, literature and philosophy'.[98] To mark the new year, 500 destitute Indians were fed by the Society at the home of J. A. Luckhoo. Cerebral as well as practical work was undertaken. Peter Ruhomon, D. Iloo, K. P. Das and K. R. Yerrakadu — the most prominent members of the East Indian

Young Men's Society — were also active in the new Society. Indo-Guyanese Christianity was refracted through an imagination suffused with the ascendant pride in India, ancient and modern.

In October 1925, at a reception in honour of Kunwar Maharaj Singh, the delegate from India who visited British Guiana in connection with the Colonisation Scheme, the East Indian Young Men's Society greeted him as a 'distinguished visitor from the Motherland'. They also underlined their communion with their ancestral home:

> As Indians we feel a justifiable pride in our Motherland and the achievements of her sons; and watch with considerable interest her social, intellectual, and political development. The many ties of interest and affection that bind us to her can never be broken; and though separated from her by miles of ocean, we are one with her in thought, one in feeling, and one in aspirations...[99]

Maharaj Singh was enamoured of the adaptability and flexibility of Indo-Guyanese :the virtual extinction of caste distinctions and their accompanying disabilities; the erosion of the taboo on inter-caste marriages. He also expressed pleasure in what he saw as 'the great freedom' which Indian women enjoyed in the colony; adding that they had an important role to play in 'the forward movement'.[100]

Indeed, women were already making a major contribution to the visible Hindu and Muslim cultural revival in the 1920s, the decade after the end of indentureship. The elaborate rituals, the lavish preparation of food associated with religious functions, the absorbing hospitality extended to visiting priests, devotees, *jahajis* (shipmates), the musical accompaniment, etc., owe much to these industrious, resilient women on the plantations and in the villages. Women achieved this while exerting much energy on their many children. When women retreat from their culture, it begins to atrophy. Indo-Guyanese women were the custodians of myriad, complex rites and rituals brought from the eastern districts of the United Provinces and western Bihar; they remain so today, in spite of the irreparable loss of their language.

It is noteworthy that the founding of the first women's organisation in British Guiana — the East Indian Ladies' Guild — in June 1927, under the presidency of Alice Bhagwandai Singh,[101] followed shortly the election to the presidency of the Indian National Congress of Mrs. Sarojini Naidu (1879-1949), the distinguished poet and politician, who had studied at Girton College, Cambridge. The British Guiana East Indian Association had extended an invitation for her to visit the colony; but she replied that the pressure of work made it impossible for her to do so. Earlier, in July 1926, Hon. A. E. Seeram, a local Indian legislator, cited the exemplary work of Mrs. Naidu, when advocating the education of Indian girls.[102]

Among the cultural events undertaken by Alice Bhagwandai Singh and the East Indian Ladies' Guild, was the production, in April 1929, of a play, 'Savitri', based on a story from the Hindu epic, the *Mahabharata*. The synopsis of the play, in the programme issued by the Guild, read:

> Maharajah Aswapati is blessed in his old age with a female heir, whom he names Savitri. Savitri falls in love with Satyavan, a prince of royal blood, who just before marriage, fought a battle in which his throne is usurped. Although she is informed that a year after marriage the prince would die, and that she would have to follow him into the forest, where his parents have exiled themselves, she there and then marries him. Satyavan does die a year afterwards, but his life is restored through the kindness of Yama [the God of the dead]. [103]

R. B. Gajraj played Aswapati; Hardutt Singh, Satyavan; I. H. Premdas, the Rishi; E. V. Luckhoo, Yama; and Miss I. Beharry Lall, Savitri. Gajraj was a Muslim; Singh, the son of Alice Bhagwandai Singh and Dr. J. B. Singh, a Hindu; and Luckhoo a Christian. This was *not* extraordinary. The principal Indian organisations in the colony — the East Indian Cricket

Club (founded 1915), the British Guiana East Indian Association (founded 1916), and the [Wesleyan] East Indian Young Men's Society (founded 1919) — at all times, comprised a broad cross-section of the Indian community. A comprehensive Indian identity, inconceivable in India, had cohered in British Guiana. Besides, the character of Savitri, like Sita in the other great Hindu epic, the *Ramayana,* is a woman whose devotion to her husband is unimpeachable. This ideal Hindu wife of boundless self-abnegation was the ideal wife of all Indian men, whatever their religion.

Jeremy Poynting argues that Alice Bhagwandai Singh and her colleagues 'possessed in an unabsurd and self-liberating way what they thought was the best of Western culture, linked always to a strong sense of pride in their distinctive cultural identity'.[104]

Another organisation which contributed significantly to Indian cultural effervescence in the 1920s was the Hindoo Society. It was founded in April 1922, during the visit of Pillai and Tivary, the delegates from India who had come to investigate the abortive Colonisation Scheme. The main aims of the Society were to impart religious and educational knowledge to Hindus, and establish a *Dharam Sala* (Home for the Poor), for destitute people in Georgetown, whatever their race or religion. Many prominent Indians, including Dr. J. B. Singh, and his wife, Alice, Mahadeo Panday, the Rev. James Persaud, an Anglican minister, and Peter Ruhomon, did useful work for the Hindoo Society; but the principal architect of its success was Pandit Ramsaroop [Maraj], an 'indefatigable worker', a selfless, efficient man. He was the trustee of the Society, and an outstanding fund-raiser. He travelled throughout the colony, patiently persuading people to contribute to the Society's work.[105]

Pandit Ramsaroop was magnanimous. An extremely tolerant Brahmin, in 1918, he gave the Methodist missionary to the Indians, Rev. H. M. Yates, a section of a building he owned for use as a church. This was a most extraordinary gesture, as his father had been the Hindu pandit in his district in south Georgetown, Albuoystown; he himself had been a trustee of the temple for several years; and Rev. Yates was trying to convert Indians in the Pandit's own backyard. Ramsaroop never converted to Christianity; but his spontaneous opening to the Methodists underlined the inviolable decency of this humble man. It is interesting that it was Rev. Yates who founded the East Indian Young Men's Society, in 1919, primarily for the intellectual uplift of young Indians in Georgetown. As noted earlier, its lectures and discussions were secular and educational, with considerable focus on India. The Methodists can be seen as responding to the generosity of spirit manifested by Pandit Ramsaroop.[106]

By 1923, a new Hindu temple was erected at James Street, Albuoystown. The officiating priest and trustee was the Pandit. In August 1926, a Hindi school was opened in the same compound; the foundation stone had been laid by the delegate from India, Kunwar Maharaj Singh, in October 1925. At the inaugural ceremonies at the school, Mahadeo Panday, the president of the Hindoo Society, observed, with regret, that many Indo-Guyanese were unable to read and write Hindi. He explained:

> ... it is not difficult to see that in the course of time, this process of denationalisation would assume large proportions; and the Indians... of this colony will lose all connection with the language and customs of their fore-fathers, and the country of their origin. We have decided to found the school in an endeavour to arrest this tendency.[107]

Governor Rodwell lauded the aims of the Hindi School. He, also, remarked that the children were growing up in ignorance of Hindi, the language which was crucial to the retention of links with India, and which 'possessed the fine traditions of the Hindus'.[108] Meanwhile, a few weeks before, in August 1926, the British Guiana East Indian Association had opened their new building in Church Street, Georgetown. A. E. Seeram, a leading member of the Association, noted that 'though separated from India by many thousands of miles, they all could say that in that building they had true and loyal sons of Mother India'.[109]

On 14 July 1929, the *Dharam Sala* (Home for the Poor) was opened by

Rev. C. F. Andrews.   At the opening function, the secretary of the Hindoo Society, Rev. James Persaud, said that all races had contributed to the construction of the two-storey building with thirty-six rooms. The cornerstone had been laid by Pandit Ramsaroop in February 1928, when the Pandit announced that the *Dharam Sala* would be opened to poor people of all races. C. F. Andrews presented to the Pandit a prayer which he had received from Rabindranath Tagore; and expressed the hope that racial harmony would prevail in British Guiana. [110]

What was most impressive about the Hindoo Society was the punctiliousness with which it stuck to its schedule for achieving clearly-defined goals. It could be argued that the visits of Pillai and Tivary in 1922, Maharaj Singh in 1925, and Rev. C. F. Andrews in 1929, galvanised the Society to execute its programme with resolution, vigour, and discipline: the approval of these distinguished visitors from the 'Motherland' seemed to have inspired them, sustaining a sense of purpose and communal responsibility. But it was the imaginative, perceptibly selfless, leadership of Pandit Ramsaroop which coaxed co-operation and solid support from a broad cross-section of the society. Peter Ruhomon, towards the end of the 1930s, memorialised the impeccable record, in the Hindoo Society, of the venerable Pandit:

> ...the soul of the movement is the Maraj himself, who brings to bear upon the work such a catholicity of outlook, a sincerity of motive, a humility of spirit, and a breath of visioning, as to have won for him a way into the heart of everyone, and laid the basis for the success of his efforts and the security of the work. [111]

In December 1941, the Hindoo Society, in welcoming the new Governor of British Guiana, proudly announced that after 'twenty years of incessant toil', it had acquired a temple, a Hindi school, a charity home in Georgetown, a *Dharam Sala,* an orphanage, a soup kitchen, an Anglican church (sic), two large sheds, a new charity home in Georgetown, a

Dharam Sala in Berbice, and a cottage in the capital, used as quarters by its officers. It was a supreme achievement; and it won official recognition: Pandit Ramsaroop Maraj was awarded the M.B.E.. [112]

From the 1920s, among Hindu, Muslim, and Christian Indians in British Guiana, a contagious spirit of renewal, of expanding self-confidence, fed by growing economic security in the colony and political and intellectual advances in India, took shape. There was an upsurge in the building of mosques and temples: some, like the mosque at Queenstown,[113] and the Hindu temple at Providence (East Bank Demerara), were, in the context of the colony, architectural achievements of considerable merit. Indo-Guyanese were, in their own minds, erasing the old scar of inferiority, the stubborn 'coolie' image; [114] they took pride in asserting their rich, cultural heritage. The visits of the *Arya Samaj* missionary, Mehta Jaimini,[115] and Gandhi's confidant and virtual disciple, Rev. C. F. Andrews, in 1929, strengthened the link, the identity of Indo-Guiana with India.

In March 1929, Jaimini addressed a mixed audience at the Town Hall, Georgetown; Percy C. Wight, the Mayor, presided. He spoke on 'The Message of Mother India'. He said that the peace, progress, and prosperity of British Guiana 'entirely rested' on the Indians; adding that if they left the colony, it would 'go to the dogs'. Jaimini quoted copiously from Max Müller, the eminent Sanskrit scholar, to underline the antiquity, richness, and profoundly civilised accomplishments of Aryan India. He then counterposed to the reservoir of spiritual wealth of contemporary India, the poverty of 'the inner life' of advanced Western civilisation: the message of India to the world was primarily one of renunciation and the simplicity of living. He admonished his Guianese listeners to spiritualise their lives, enriching them by cultivating selflessness; not to become mired in the emptiness of materialism.

Jaimini added that Gandhi's life of 'self-abnegation' was a lesson for the world; and that his simplicity, austerity, renunciation, and purity of motives had made him a saint. That was the message of India: there would be an end to wars when Gandhi's vision was assimilated universally.[116]

Jaimini addressed Indians throughout British Guiana, on aspects of Indian history and culture, making lavish claims for India: 'the cradle of civilisation', 'the basis of western philosophy', 'the fountainhead of religion'.[117] In his lecture to the [Wesleyan] East Indian Young Men's Society, he appealed to them to 'take pride in the high culture and civilisation of immense antiquity of their own country', India.[118]

C. F. Andrews arrived in the colony as Jaimini was immersed in his lectures. The British Guiana East Indian Association had received a telegram from Benarsidas Chaturvedi of the Indian National Congress on Andrews's visit: 'Leaving out Mahatma Gandhi, he is the only man in India whose words carry the greatest weight with the Indian public on the question of Indians abroad. Gandhi considers him as his younger brother, and has given him the name "Deena Bandhu" — "friend of the poor". Please see that he gets all information that he wants'. The British Guiana East Indian Association advised Indo-Guyanese that it was 'their duty to support the Congress and entertain the visitor'.[119]

Andrews spent over three months in British Guiana, in 1929. He visited numerous villages and plantations, and addressed the members of many organisations throughout the colony.[120] The residents of Windsor Forest, West Coast Demerara, presented their eminent guest with an address. It epitomised the feelings of Indians in British Guiana towards the 'motherland', at the end of the 1920s; the villagers were requesting a new system of immigration from India, to augment their numbers, and reinvigorate their cultural heritage:

> We trust that God will grant you to be the fountainhead from which will spring... a new system of scientific emigration, to the general good of British Guiana and Mother India... In the preservation of the languages and literature of Mother India lies our hope.
> In the loss of connection with India and its literature, we fear the disintegration of the best national trait and character of our people. We take pride in the cherished customs, ideals, and traditions of Mother

India and this, in our humble opinion, can only be preserved by the infusing of new blood from the Mother Country.[121]

It was as if every achievement, every action, had to be assessed against a transcendent moral entity — the feelings of 'Mother India'.

VI

IN THE SHADOW OF 'MOTHER INDIA':
THE LIMITATIONS OF INDO-GUYANESE POLITICS

In estimating the value of the factors at work in shaping the new outlook, nationalism must not be ignored. The coming of goodwill missionaries from India and Official Delegates from the Indian Government has played an important part in the national awakening. There is now a growing pride in the consciousness of race and the cultural heritage that has been bequeathed to them.

Peter Ruhomon, *Centenary History of the East Indians in British Guiana, 1838-1938* (Georgetown: The East Indians 150th Anniversary Committee, 1988 [1947]), p. 288.

By the end of the 1920s even Samuel Lupton, the editor of *The Daily Argosy*, was able to acknowledge the elevation of Gandhi to virtual saint-hood among Indo-Guyanese. In March 1929, he wrote, somewhat repent-antly:

It must be understood that I accept the purity of motives of Mr. Gan-dhi. No Englishman in India has ever questioned them, or failed to reverence his asceticism and austere honesty of character. The charge against Mr. Gandhi has never been that he is not sincere or high-minded. On the contrary, it is declared that he is a misguided saint, or rather a saint whose idealistic doctrines are distorted or perverted by politicians who use Mr. Gandhi as a tool.[122]

To the Indians in the colony, the nationalist struggle in India was theirs. Indeed, as argued earlier, local Indian issues were constantly refracted through a sensibility moulded by a resurgent pride in the 'motherland', and their perceived duty to her. (This was accelerated in the 1930s - 1940s). The Indian Centenary Number of *The Daily Chronicle* (5 May 1938), to commemorate 100 years of the Indian presence in British Guiana, commenced with *Bande Mataram*, 'the proposed national anthem of India'. C. R. Jacob, the president of the British Guiana East Indian Association, in his centenary address of May 1938, underlined the profound influence which India had on the Indo-Guyanese imagination; and striking a rich, idyllic, Indian vein, he dreamt big:

> ....we see lines of communication established between the colony and Mother India and new blood infiltrating in our communal arteries, keeping alive the cultural heritage of a glorious past and inspiring us to newer adventures...
>
> The vision of our beloved Tagore of a 'New India', is the ideal towards which we are also striving in the Greater India we hope to build in the Colony...[123]

This unambiguous identification with a 'New India', seen to be in revolt against alien rule and reclaiming/reshaping itself, strengthened Indians in the colony psychologically. It linked them with the legacy of a great, ancient tradition. It also inspired hopes for the future, for the freedom of India, which until the rise of their own leader, Cheddi Jagan, after 1947, Indo-Guyanese, in an instinctive, millennial way, interpreted as conterminous with their own freedom, their dignity — an elemental act of repossession; a catharsis (see Appendix VIII).

This solid identity with 'Mother India', however, was accompanied by some negative repercussions for the political development of Indians in British Guiana. It prolonged a sense of ambivalence towards the colony, even among creolised, Christian Indians. It delayed the emergence of a comprehensive, unmediated loyalty to British Guiana. A vacillating, frequently petty, leadership survived well into the 1940s: they seemed to be perpetually looking over their shoulders for 'Mother India's' guidance and reassurance. Above all it encouraged the Indo-Guyanese leadership to ignore the feelings of the Afro-Guyanese, and the political, economic and cultural space this group was also demanding.

The issue of the appointment of an agent general from India, as a custodian of Indo-Guyanese rights, underscored both the depth of the dependence and the extend to which these interests were defined almost solely in ethnic terms. In March 1922, for instance, the Indian residents of Bush Lot Village, West Coast Berbice, in an address to Pillai and Tivary, the delegates from India, requested that professionals from India, lawyers and doctors, be sent to the colony to represent them. They envisaged that 'These men could be the eyes of India on the people here and those to come, so as to safeguard their rights'. As they explained:

> ... the native-born professional men cannot, and will never, have the sentiment and affection as a true-born Indian would towards his race. East Indians in the colony, who have reached the top of the ladder... intellectually and financially, have often-times neglected to fight the cause of their brethren, simply for the smile of another race.[124]

Even J. A. Luckhoo, the first Indian legislator in British Guiana, at the hearings of the Colonisation Committee, in 1922, endorsed the suggestion that a representative from India be sent to the colony to represent Indian plantation workers. He said:

> ... I do not think they were sufficiently represented by the Immigration Department of this Colony. The Immigration Agent General is known as the Protector of East Indians, but although known by that name, I do not think that in practice he carries out the duties devolv-

ing on him ... It would require an Indian really to go into the feelings of the immigrants ... We ought to have here a member of the Indian race, from India, as the Immigration Agent General.[125]

It was this stubborn inferiority complex in political affairs, and the notion that 'Mother India' would/should protect them, which contributed to their failure to form a trade union for plantation workers, and the chaotic state of industrial relations on sugar estates, culminating in the shootings at Ruimveldt in April 1924.[126] The Afro-Guyanese, by contrast, had no such concrete attachment to their ancestral Africa; their 'motherland' was British Guiana; they demonstrated greater political maturity: they formed the British Guiana Labour Union in 1919; were deeply involved in local government; and were acquiring political sophistication in other spheres. As late as 1938, the president of the British Guiana East Indian Association, Hon. C. R. Jacob, a member of the Legislative Council, advocated the appointment of an agent general for British Guiana, from India, as recommended to the Governor-General of India by the Indian Legislative Council.[127] During the Indian centenary celebrations, in May 1938, another member of the British Guiana East Indian Association, J. A. Luckhoo, moved a motion 'to secure the appointment of an Agent of the Government of India to protect the interests, particularly economic and educational, of the Indian residents of the Colony...' An agent general from India was considered superior because of 'his knowledge of the psychology of the Indian people'.[128] In early 1939, this resolution was incorporated into the memorandum which the Association submitted to the Moyne Commission. [129]

It is interesting that this hankering after what seemed like an omniscient protector from 'Mother India', was being articulated even when Indo-Guyanese representation in the legislature was on the increase. In the general elections of 1935, four were elected. However, the long shadow of India stretched far: the nationalist struggle inspired and constrained.

In 1927, the Colonial Office was manoeuvring to replace the representative constitution of British Guiana by Crown Colony government: this involved the subordination of the elective principle to the nominated. The leaders of the British Guiana East Indian Association were incensed by what they saw as a retrograde step, and were among the most vocal campaigners against Crown Colony government. But the long shadow of India hovered, eclipsing the imagination of Indo-Guyanese leaders.

In early August 1927, for instance, the Association issued a circular against a rival, splinter organisation, the Indian Congress of British Guiana; the latter was considered to be sympathetic to Crown Colony Government. The Association advised all Indo-Guyanese: 'Bear in mind that Mahatma Gandhi, Mrs. Sarojini Naidu, Pandit Motilal Nehru, Pandit Malaviya, and the late C. R. Das have always chosen for (sic) responsible Government. What would India say if you do not do likewise?'[130]

The secretary of the British Guiana East Indian Association, Ayube Edun, in a letter of 2 September 1927, to H. S. L. Polak of the Indians Overseas Association for transmission to the Secretary of State for India, argued that under the constitution Indians enjoyed complete equality. The Association observed: 'He is very much a citizen, and there is no barrier to his progress politically, economically, socially or religiously...' They added that 'through sheer dint (sic) and perseverance and with the help of a liberal constitution', Indians in British Guiana had become professionals, merchants, traders, large landed proprietors, agriculturalists, 'with immense stake' in the colony. They were apprehensive that Crown Colony government would undermine their achievements, rendering their situation worse than that of their compatriots in Kenya, South Africa, and Fiji.[131]

Indo-Guyanese leaders hoped that their 'Motherland' would take a keen interest in their welfare, that she would protect them:

> Our Association feels that India should, in no uncertain voice, demand a hearing in the interest of her people in British Guiana. We hope and look out for a gleam of light from the Motherland. Her leaders should stretch out a hand of consolation to her benighted sons

and daughters across the seas. In this crisis the Motherland should
never forsake us.[132]

Then, in a contradictory vein, they pointed out that the crux of the problem was that a small European minority in the colony was seeking to conserve its privileges, because they feared that 'Indians and Negroes will, in
the near future, rule British Guiana'. They implored: 'It is for the Leaders
of the Motherland to act and act quickly... The Motherland has championed
the cause successfully of her children in South Africa. British Guiana's dark
day is at hand, and we look to her for help'.[133] But Edun and his colleagues
anticipated Indian domination in British Guiana. It was not clear how this
was reconcilable with Indian and Afro-Guyanese 'rule' in the colony:

> The consensus of opinion, in well-considered Indian circles, is that in
> the near future we shall dominate the political situation. With our
> 42% of population, our influence must be felt — it is the natural
> sequence of things when our people are realising the true meaning of
> the franchise.[134]

On 3 January 1928, the executive committee of the Association wrote to
the acting Governor of British Guiana, stating that in view of discrimina-
tion against Indians in other colonies, they were apprehensive of what con-
stitutional change meant for their long-term security. They said that India
had been 'awakened by the cry of immigrants from colonies desiring to
return to the Motherland'; and claimed that they had received information
that the Government of Gwalior, in Central India, had reserved a large area
for returning immigrants, with substantial facilities for agricultural settle-
ments. The British Guiana East Indian Association concluded that they had
not informed Indians in the colony of this; but that if Crown Colony government were imposed, they would not only disseminate this information,
but would advise 'all self-respecting' Indians to leave British Guiana.[135]
(On 18 July 1928, the 1891 Constitution was revoked. Crown Colony gov-

ernment was imposed. Business continued as usual).

Mass repatriation was probably a desperate, limp threat; yet it dramatised the extent to which Gandhian India had fired the Indo-Guyanese imagination, but, in the process, contained their thoughts and vision within its own procrustean mould. Moreover, the resurgence of pride in their Indian heritage delayed the emergence of a comprehensive identity with the colony.

Nehru, unwittingly, contributed to the sustaining of this indecisive, often unimaginative, leadership. In 1927, as secretary of the All-India Congress Committee, he had advised: 'An Indian who goes to other countries must co-operate with the people of that country and win for himself a position of friendship and service...'[136] In 1937, Nehru tied the fate of Indians abroad, totally and unambiguously, to the freedom of India. It becomes possible to comprehend the British Guiana East Indian Association's tactless 'Greater India' exhortation, in May 1938, against Nehru's definitive prescription of 1937:

> Our countrymen abroad must realise that the key to their problems lies in India. They rise or they fall with the rise and fall of India. If India lives and is free, they live and we live.[137]

But if the attachment to India constrained the Indo-Guyanese response to a Guyana moving towards the end of colonialism, it also sustained them through oppressive times, then and in the years ahead. It also ensured that the Indo-Guyanese held on to a cultural heritage which could, in time, enrich Guyanese society as a whole.

This was recognised by some far-seeing observers in this period. In 1936, for instance, the head of the Canadian Mission in British Guiana, the Rev. J. B. Cropper, retired after forty years (1896-1936) of solid work in the education of Indians. He recalled that while he always aimed at building an Indian Presbyterian Church, he believed it was essential to 'conserve the genius of the East': '... the East Indian had a genius which should not be Westernised'.[138] Cropper did not win many converts to Christianity; but his enduring empathy with aspects of the Indian tradition percolated through his schools, making it possible for some of his Indo-Guyanese students to 'discover' India.

Jawaharlal Nehru has written that the great epics of India, the *Ramayana* and the *Mahabharata*, possessed the imagination of ordinary folk: 'every incident and story and moral in them was engraved on the popular mind... the illiterate peasant had a picture gallery in his mind... [which] was largely drawn from myth and tradition and epic heroes and heroines, and only very little from history'. Nehru juxtaposes this popular construct with his own picture of India, shaped by 'recorded history and more-or-less ascertained fact', assigning credibility to both.[139]

In Guyana, too, these two constructs of India have co-existed since the 1890s. Wherever Indo-Guyanese live today — in derelict Guyana or in the second diaspora: New York, Toronto, London, etc. — visions of India will not leave them. These, often, are folk images — eclectic, largely mythical, constructs compounded of idyllic impressions moulded by the heroic tales of the *Ramayana*, in particular; and the synthetic images of splendour and triumphalism, fed by fifty years of Bombay movies; combined with smatterings of the 'more-or-less' historical India of Max Müller, Joseph Ruhomon, and Nehru. But, embedded in these extravagant, surreal, liquid images of India, are solid, sustaining notions of industry, thrift, ambition, commitment to family, self-respect, and communion with a transcendent, divine sphere, encapsulated in timeless, but malleable, 'Mother India'. To Indo-Guyanese, this India of the imagination is real; it instructs, inspires, and sustains them; it lightens the darkness.

APPENDIX I

Warren Hastings on Indology (1784)

Every accumulation of knowledge, and especially such as is obtained by social communication with people over whom we exercise a dominion founded on the right of conquest, is useful to the State; it is the gain of humanity ... it attracts and conciliates distant affections; it lessens the weight of the chain by which the natives are held in subjection; and it imprints on the hearts of our own countrymen the sense and obligation of benevolence. Even in England, this effect of it is greatly wanting. It is not very long since the inhabitants of India were considered by many as creatures scarce elevated above the degree of savage life; nor, I fear, is that prejudice yet wholly eradicated, though surely abated. Every instance which brings their real character home to observation will impress us with a more generous feeling for their natural rights, and teach us to estimate them by the measure of our own. But such instances can only be obtained in their writings: and these will survive when the British Dominion in India shall have long ceased to exist, and when the sources which it once yielded of wealth and power are lost to remembrance.

Introduction to Charles Wilkins's translation of the *Bhagavad Gita (1784)*, quoted in Penderel Moon, *Warren Hastings and British India* (London: Hodder and Stoughton, 1947), pp. 352-353.

APPENDIX II

Max Müller on Ram Mohan Roy's Rebellious Spirit (1883)

There was everything to induce Rammohun [sic] Roy to retain the religion of his fathers. It was an ancient religion, a national religion, and allowed an independent thinker greater freedom than almost any other religion. But openly to condemn and reject that religion, or at least its present form, involved more serious consequences in India than almost anywhere else. It entailed not only censure and punishment, and the loss of the love of his parents; it entailed loss of caste, expulsion from society, loss of prosperity. All this Rammohun Roy was prepared to face; and he had to face it. He was banished from his father's house once or twice; he was insulted by his friends; his life was threatened, and even in the streets of Calcutta he had to walk about armed. Later in life his relations (his own mother) tried to deprive him of his caste, and indirectly of his property, and it was a mere accident that the law decided in his favour.

.... during all these struggles, and when he was left almost alone, he did not join any other community where, as a convert, he might have been received with open arms and warm hearts. He never became a Mohammedan, he never became a Christian, but he remained to the end a Brahman, a believer in the Veda, and in the One God who, as he maintained, had been revealed in the Veda, and especially in the Vedanta, long before he revealed himself in the Bible or in the Koran.

He wished to reform his religion, not to reject it. His mother, we are told, was for a time broken-hearted about her son. It was she who, after the death of her eldest son ... brought an action against Rammohun Roy to disinherit him as an apostate and infidel. But her son had the satisfaction, later in life, to hear from her own loving lips words which must have consoled him for many sorrows. 'Son', she said to him, a year before her death, 'you are right. But I am a weak woman, and am grown too old to give up those observances which are a comfort to me'.

... a man who is ready to sacrifice everything for the voice of truth, who submits to be called a sceptic, a heretic, an atheist, even by his dearest friends, is an unselfish, an honest, a bold man...

He would not say that he believed in three gods, when he believed in One God only; he would not call idols symbols of the Godhead; he would not allow Suttee [sati or the immolation of widows] because it was a time-hallowed custom, springing from the true love of a wife for a dead husband. He would have no compromising, no economising, no playing with words, no shifting of responsibility from his own shoulders to others. And therefore, whatever narrow-minded critics may say, I say once more that Rammohun Roy was an unselfish, an honest, a bold man — a great man in the highest sense of the word.

F. Max Müller, *Biographical Essays* (London: Longmans, Green, and Co., 1884), pp. 32-35.

APPENDIX III

Max Müller on India's Aryan Antecedents (1859)

... though the Brahmans of India belong to the same family, the Aryan or Indo-European family, which civilised the whole of Europe, the two great branches of that primitive race were kept asunder for centuries after their first separation. The main stream of the Aryan nations has always flowed towards the northwest ... Few will stay behind when all are going. But to let one's friends depart, and then to set out ourselves — to take a road which, lead where it may, can never lead us to join those again who speak our language and worship our gods — is a course which only men of strong individuality and great self-dependence are capable of pursuing. It was the course adopted by the southern branch of the Aryan family, the Brahmanic Aryans of India and the Zoroastrians of Iran [the Parsees].

At the first dawn of traditional history, we see these Aryan tribes migrating across the snow of the Himalaya, toward the 'Seven Rivers' (the Indus, the five rivers of the Panjab and the Sarasvati), and ever since India has been called their home. That before that time they had been living in more northern regions, within the same precincts with the ancestors of the Greeks, the Italians, Slavonians, Germans, and Celts, is a fact as firmly established as that the Normans of William the Conqueror were the Northmen of Scandinavia. The evidence of language is irrefragable, and it is the only evidence worth listening to with regard to ante-historical periods. It would have been next to impossible to discover any traces of relationship between the swarthy natives of India and their conquerors, whether Alexander or Clive, but for the testimony borne by language. What other evidence could have reached back to times when Greece was not peopled by Greeks nor India by Hindus?... What authority would have been strong enough to persuade the Grecian army, that their gods and their hero ancestors were the same as those of King Porus, or to convince the English soldier that the same blood was running in his veins and in the veins of the dark Bengalese [sic]? And yet there is not an English jury nowadays, which, after examining the hoary documents of language, would reject the claim of a common descent and a legitimate relationship between Hindu, Greek, and Teuton. Many words still live in India and in England, that have witnessed the first separation of the northern and southern Aryans ... The terms for God, for house, for father, mother, son, daughter, for dog and cow, for heart and tears, for axe and tree, identical in all the Indo-European idioms, are like the watchwords of soldiers. We challenge the seeming stranger; and whether he answers with the lips of a Greek, a German, or an Indian, we recognise him as one of ourselves... There *was* a time when the ancestors of the Celts, the Germans, the Slavonians, the Greeks, and Italians, the Persians, and Hindus, were living together within the same fences, separate from the ancestors of the Semitic and Turanian races.

F Max Müller, *A History of Ancient Sanskrit Literature so far as it Illustrates the Primitive Religion of the Brahmans* (London: Williams and Norgate, 1859), pp. 12-14.

APPENDIX IV

Max Müller: 'What can India Teach Us?' (1882)

Take any of the burning questions of the day — popular education, higher education, parliamentary representation, codification of laws, finance, emigration, poor-law, and whether you have anything to teach and to try, or anything to observe and to learn, India will supply you with a laboratory such as exists nowhere else. That very Sanskrit, the study of which may at first seem so tedious to you and so useless, if only you will carry it on ... will open before you large layers of literature, as yet almost unknown and unexplored, and allow you an insight into strata of thought deeper than any you have known before, and rich in lessons that appeal to the deepest sympathies of the human heart.

F. Max Müller, *India, What can it Teach Us?: A Course of Lectures Delivered Before the University of Cambridge [1882]* (London: Longmans, Green, and Co., 1883), pp. 13-14.

APPENDIX V

The British Guiana East Indian Institute's Letter of Congratulations to Dadabhai Naoroji, the first Indian M.P. in Britain (October 1892)

British Guiana
Georgetown, Demerara

1 October 1892

Hon. Dada Bhai [sic] Naoroji, M.P., London

Sir, — We, the undersigned members of the British Guiana East Indian Institute, having learnt with exceeding joy and gratification of your election as a member of the House of Parliament of Great Britain, deem it not only an honour but a duty of our race in this remote part of Her Majesty's dominions, to tender you our unanimous and most hearty congratulations for the distinguished position you have achieved.

We are fully conscious of the multifarious difficulties you must necessarily have had to surmount in order to secure your success in this, to our nation, memorable election, and that fact alone impels us to doubly prize the honour which the East Indian Nation has, through your meritorious instrumentality, attained — an event unparalleled in the annals of the History of India.

We need hardly say that although we are thousands of miles separated from you, it will be our foremost interest to read of your career, and earnestly trust that success will attend your undertakings both politically and otherwise, and we further venture to hope that the example which you have so nobly set will be fruitful in actuating others of our ancient race to follow; and thereby rid themselves and countrymen of the political oblivion which they have been presumed hitherto to be sunk.

In concluding our humble quota of the many manifestations of pride at your entrance into such a traditionally illustrious house, which you have already received from well-wishers in other parts of the globe, we fervently hope that Almighty God will direct your every movement in your elevated sphere, and thereby ensure a brilliant and happy career for one in whose veins courses our kindred blood.

We have the honour to be,
Sir,
Your obedient Servants,

Golab C. Bezbaroa, L.R.C.P. (Edinburgh), L.F.P.S. (Glasgow), president; Veerasammy Mudhai [sic] [Mudaliar], vice-president; F. E. Jaundoo, treasurer; J. R. Wharton, honorary secretary; Thomas Flood.

The Daily Chronicle, 7 October 1892.

[William Hewley Wharton's name is, inexplicably, absent from the reported signatories of the letter. In his biographical entry in *Who is Who in British Guiana, 1945-1948* (Georgetown: The Daily Chronicle Ltd., 1948), p. 551, he is cited as having 'founded', in 1892, the B. G. East Indian Institute — 'the first Society of East Indians formed in the Caribbean'. In that year he was a chemist and druggist in British Guiana. He left for the University of Edinburgh in 1893].

APPENDIX VI

Indo-Guyanese and the Coronation of King George V:
Address of Loyalty (May 1911)

There was a large gathering of East Indians in the Town Hall, Georgetown, on Thursday evening [18 May 1911], when a meeting was held for the purpose of subscribing to a Coronation Address to be forwarded to Their Majesties, King George and Queen Mary.

Dr. [William Hewley] Wharton took the chair, and he was supported on the platform by a large number of East Indians, among whom were the Rev. [James] Persaud, Dr. Ram [Narain] Sharma, Messrs. Thomas Flood, James Wharton, Baboo Ram Sawh, and Pandit [Parmanand] Saraswat.

In introducing the chairman to the meeting, Mr. Flood said they had gathered together to make arrangements for celebrating the Coronation of a great King. He thought it was their duty, considering the advantages they enjoyed under British rule, to send a loyal Address to King George and Queen Mary, and he was very glad to see so many East Indians present.

Dr. Wharton... said... [it] was a very great occasion in the history of British Guiana, and, so far as he knew, it was the first occasion upon which a body of East Indians had met... to send an Address to a Royal Sovereign. ... The object of the meeting they all understood. They had an informal meeting at the residence of Mr. Thomas Flood, the meeting being held at the suggestion of Mr. James Wharton ... it was decided that a public meeting should be held to draw up a suitable Address to King George, the King of Great Britain and Ireland, Defender of the Faith, and also Emperor of India. (Applause). It was as the Emperor of India that they had met there to do him honour. He had no doubt that they were all, like himself, loyal subjects of the King. (Applause).

Some of them had come from different parts of India, and others, like himself, had been born of native parents in British Guiana; but they all knew full well the advantages, privileges, and kindnesses experienced in this country; and if it had not been for the benign influence of the Emperor of India, he did not think they would have received such privileges and advantages. They were enjoying privileges which were not enjoyed by their ancestors. They had no fear, as they knew they were protected by the British law, and the same privileges were meted out to them as the Englishmen.

The Rev. Mr. Persaud said... [in] December this year there would be another Coronation of the King at the Durbar at Delhi, and so it was a nice thing to send a memorial now, as when the King would be leaving the English shore to go to India, he would feel that he had the hearts and sentiment of the East Indians in South America with him.

... Dr. Sharma... referred to the progress India had made under British rule; and asked those present to attach their signatures, and subscribe to defray whatever expenses might be incurred.

... The Chairman then called on Mr. James Wharton to read the Address.

THE ADDRESS

> To His Most Excellent Majesty King George V, by the Grace of God, King of the United Kingdom of Great Britain and Ireland and of the British Dominions beyond the Seas, Defender of the Faith, Emperor of India and Her Most Gracious Majesty Queen Mary.

May it please Your Majesties, — We, the undersigned East Indians, residing in the colony of British Guiana who constitute no less than one-third of the population thereof, for ourselves and on behalf of our fellow countrymen, have the honour most humbly and respectfully to tender to Your Majesties our most heartfelt and sincerest congratulations upon Your accession to the Royal Throne not only as King of Great Britain and the

Dominions beyond the Seas, but more particularly as Emperor of India, a possession which we feel assured Your Majesties regard as one of the brightest jewels in the Imperial Crown.

Situated as we are thousands of miles away from our fatherland, and from Your Majesties' home, we feel that we cannot permit this auspicious occasion to pass without recording our genuine and humble loyalty to the Throne — a loyalty which we have the honour and privilege to assure Your Majesties not only exists today but is as unwavering in its fervency and constancy of nature as it was during the reign of Your late lamented parent, King Edward VII, whose memory we cherish along with that of Your revered grandmother, Queen Victoria, first Empress of India, the effect of whose benign reigns India and her sons amidst all races and climes regard as epoch-making in their history.

We most respectfully ask Your Majesties' acceptance of this our humble conveyance of congratulation, and we sincerely pray that Almighty God will in His Omnipotence grant both Your Majesties a long, a glorious and a peaceful reign and that He may extend to you that privilege of health and strength which alone can enable you to sustain the arduous duties and responsibilities which must henceforward fall upon Your Royal shoulders.

We have the honour to be, with profoundest veneration, Your Majesties' most humble and obedient servants:

Jas. Persaud, Thos. Flood, W. Hewley Wharton, Donald Gravesande, R. Premdas, Isaac Chester, Veerasawmy Mudalyar, J. Subryan, E. A. Luckhoo, Samuel Saywack, Ram Narain Sharma, Gajraj, Joshua Ramphul, Abdool Ruhomon, Parbhu Sawh, J. E. R. Ramdeholl, Pandit Kuldeep, Nadirally Khan, Beharry Lall, J. R. Wharton.

The Daily Chronicle, 20 May 1911.

Mr. James R. Wharton, the convenor of the East Indian Coronation Address Committee, forwarded to His Excellency the Governor, a few days [ago], the Address of loyalty subscribed to by the representative East Indians of the colony...

It is noticeable from the signatures that the Address is highly representative of the three Counties ... [it is] handsomely embellished in gold, with the Royal Coat of Arms together with the Colony's motto, and framed by Messrs. Mehler and Co., the well-known furnishers in colony wood.

... the Governor has despatched the Address by the Mail leaving today.

The Daily Chronicle, 28 May 1911.

APPENDIX VII

Pandit Parmanand Saraswat on Ancient India (January 1911)

In the Town Hall, Georgetown, on Thursday evening [12 January 1911], Pandit Parmanand Saraswat delivered an interesting lecture on 'Ancient India' to a crowded audience consisting principally of East Indians. Mr. James Rodway presided, and there were also on the platform Dr. W. W. Campbell, Hon. W. C. Crawford, Rev. J. Dingwall, and Messrs. [Dr] W. [Hewley] Wharton, Thomas Flood, J. Madhoo, and Veerasawmy [Mudaliar], and in the hall Ven. Archdeacon Josa and Rev. R. L. Macnie.

WHAT INDIA HAS TAUGHT [RODWAY]

The Chairman [James Rodway, an Englishman, the historian of British Guiana] said ancient India was interesting not only to the Hindoo but to Europeans, and Professor Max Müller had written a book entitled *What can India Teach Us?* India had taught Europe a great deal, and he would mention one simple thing that she had taught. The old Greeks and Romans were very sharp in a great many things, but they knew nothing about Arithmetic, nothing about the cipher or the nought; and on account of not having the nought, they could not carry on commercial business. About the year 1200, the Arabs brought to Europe figures up to 10 from India, and from that time Europe began to become mercantile. The basis of mercantile calculation, the decimal system, came from India. Another thing India had given, was still giving and would give to the world, and that was the basis of its religion, the basis of humanity — loving kindness. No people in the world were like the Hindoos for their loving kindness: the mother and father to the child, the husband to the wife, the whole family to their domestic animals....

THE LECTURE [PANDIT PARMANAND]

... What had India contributed to the world? He would give the answer in the words of Professor Max Müller, which was to the effect that if India had played no part in the political struggles of mankind, in battles or wars or the building of Empires, it had certainly the right to claim its share in the religious history of mankind... India was THE MOTHER OF RELIGI-OUS THOUGHT [sic].

... in the eighteenth century European people went to India and began to know of the Sanscrit [sic] ... a language rich in drama, literature, poetry, and philosophy ... The science of the different languages dated from the discovery of the Sanscrit; and the focus of the words mother, father, sister, etc., bore so much likeness that the conclusion to be drawn was that all the languages must have come from one original home.

The [Rig] Veda, the oldest book of mankind, was believed to have been the revelation of God, having no beginning or end ... The Veda gave a conception of God entirely different from that given elsewhere. It does not give the conception that God is a living being who knows and sees; but that He is love, knowledge, purity, and bliss Himself. Not that He is eternal happiness, but that He is happiness Himself. God as represented in the Veda was not a king or despot, sitting at a certain place, but that He was wisdom itself, and that all that came to them through nature came to them through His manifestations in different forms. There was the conception of one Godhead, one supreme being who manifested Himself in different forms ...

[Parmanand] discussed the later history of India, when the people of India influenced humanity through the Persians, Greeks, and Arabians, and when India exerted her influence through Buddhism; and said seven centuries before Christ, the standard of morality was so high, they did not require locks to their doors, did not lie, and were sober and industrious.... After discussing the teaching of Buddhism and comparing it with the teaching of Christianity, he said that they should not force the East Indians to accept the latter religion, but should educate them and make them better citizens... he appealed to East Indians to make an effort — as education was the only thing to better their condition — for the education of the rising generation.

The Daily Chronicle, 14 December 1911.

APPENDIX VIII

Excerpts from the Address by the British Guiana East Indian Association to the Delegates from India (February 1922)

At the Town Hall [Georgetown], last evening, the British Guiana East Indian Association welcomed the deputation from the Indian Government to investigate local conditions in connection with the Colonisation Scheme. The members of the deputation are Diwan Bahadur Pattu Kesava Pillai, Deputy President of the Madras Legislative Council, Mr. V. N. Tivary, member of the Servants of India Society, and Mr. G. F. Keatinge ... until recently Director of Agriculture in the Bombay Presidency. The hall was taxed to its utmost capacity, East Indians from all parts of the colony attending. Scores were unable to gain admittance.

...Among those on the platform besides the delegates were His Excellency the Governor, Sir Wilfred Collet ... Dr. W. Hewley Wharton, Honorary President of the Association, who presided, His Lordship Bishop Galton, Hons. J. Hampden King, acting Colonial Secretary, Hector Josephs, acting Attorney General ... [and] the Revs. Dr. J. B. Cropper and H. M. Yates ...

THE ADDRESS

[It was read by the secretary of the Association, K. P. Das].

Gentlemen, — We, the undersigned members of the British Guiana East Indian Association, on behalf of the said Association, and ... representing the majority of the East Indians of British Guiana, extend to you a hearty welcome in our midst.

... We desire to express our heartfelt thanks to the late revered Mr. Gokhale and other Indian patriots that the vicious system of indenture under which our forefathers were brought to these shores, a system that emasculated their manhood and destroyed the sanctity of their home-life, has been terminated, and a dark chapter in our local history, to which we look back with unqualified disgust, has been forever closed. Now we stand ´on the threshold of a new and brighter era in our history.

Numerically we are in striking preponderance to the other races of the colony. Our present number is estimated at 135,000, or about 45 per cent of the total population, located at various centres of the colony and engaged primarily in agricultural pursuits. We also have representations in the learned professions, in commerce, and the trades, as well as in the Civil Service. With regard to educational requirements, there is a slight awakening in the life of our community in recent years. A good many of our children are attending not only the primary but also the secondary schools, and are giving satisfactory account of themselves.

As members of the community in general, with whom we live in harmony and good fellowship, we are also pleased to state that we enjoy equal political and municipal rights and the other privileges of British Citizenship, as well as freedom in the exercise of our religious rites and practices.

.... [The rice industry] was inaugurated without Government aid, solely by some of our time-expired brethren, and is now second in importance to sugar. But we regret to state, it has not been given the support it deserves at the hands of the Government, for through the lack of a proper system of drainage and irrigation, serious losses have been and are still being suffered by the farmers in times of drought and during the rainy seasons.

... the rice industry affords employment to the majority of our people, and is one of the chief sources of their economic welfare ... its success or failure ... mean[s] the success or failure of the East Indian community.

NEW CHAPTER IN HISTORY

... Your coming in our midst today, initiates a new chapter in our history. Hitherto, the feeling had existed that the bond of kinship which held us to the Motherland, was broken on our migration to those distant shores.

Today we feel that we would not be left alone to work out our own salvation, but along with our kinfolks in the homeland, with whom we are one in thought, one in feeling, and one in aspirations, we would advance to a fuller sense of freedom and achieve a greater measure of success than has been vouchsafed to us in the past.

We hail, then, your coming amongst us and desire you to express to our brethren, on your return home, our deep appreciation of their kindly interest on our behalf, which we hope will hereafter be continued.

We are mindful of the great destiny that the future holds for the Motherland — the cradle of human intelligence and the guardian of Aryan wisdom — towards which she is gradually progressing.

With the attainment of complete Home Rule by India, the initial stages of which have already been granted, in redemption of the sacred pledge given under the great Charter of our late revered Queen-Empress, Victoria, and more recently reiterated by our beloved King-Emperor, George V, we hope, along with a free and awakened Motherland, to march onward, and still onward until we shall have achieved our rightful position amongst the great nations of the world ...

We have the honour to be,
Gentlemen,
Very respectfully yours,

[Signed] W. Hewley Wharton, Hony. President;
F. Kawall, Vice-President; Abdool Rayman, Vice-President; C. R. Jacob, Treasurer; Jas. Viapree, Bissoon Dyal, C. A. McDoom, P. A. Iloo, Sase Narayan, and Ramsaroop Maraj, Members of Committee; V. Kawall, Assistant Secretary; and K. P. Das, Hony. Secretary.

The Daily Argosy, 16 February 1922.

NOTES

1. For a discussion of the enduring influence of the *Ramayana* on Indo-Guyanese, see my *Indians in British Guiana, 1919-1929: A Study in Effort and Achievement* (Leeds: Peepal Tree Books/University of Warwick, forthcoming), Chapter 1, Part V.

2. H. V. P. Bronkhurst, *The Colony of British Guyana and its Labouring Population* (London: T. Woolmer, 1883), pp. 459-460.

3. Edgar Mittelholzer, *A Swarthy Boy* (London: Putnam, 1963), p. 155.

4. S. N. Mukherjee extolls Jones's seminal role in winning European recognition for Sanskrit literature; thus conferring on the Indian educated elite a sense of its own illustrious antecedents. He writes:

   ...[Jones]... presented his theories about Indian civilization in a dramatic way, which infectiously spread the romantic fascination of India and her culture throughout Europe. He and his Society evolved a methodology for the study of Indian history. His publication of *Shakuntala* and the *Gita Govinda* put Indian literature on the world map. After this no one could deny its merits.... Jones's *Shakuntala* gave them [Indians] a Shakespeare in Kalidasa...

   Sir William Jones: A Study in Eighteenth-Century British Attitudes to India (Cambridge: Cambridge University Press, 1968), pp. 121, 140.

5. David Kopf, a historian of the Bengal renaissance, explains the promptings behind Warren Hastings's promotion of Indology, an intellectual scrutiny of the Indian condition:

   ...(he) was predisposed toward a new cultural policy in which he aimed at creating an Orientalised service elite competent in Indian languages and responsive to Indian traditions. Indianisation should be conducted thenceforth not only on the level of social intercourse but also on that of intellectual exchange... the

Englishman would have to think and act like an Asian. Otherwise, the British would be treated as aliens, rapport between ruler and ruled would break down, and the Empire would ultimately collapse.
British Orientalism and the Bengal Renaissance: The Dynamics of Indian Modernization, 1773-1835 (Berkeley: University of California Press, 1969), pp. 17-18.

6. Mukherjee, *op. cit.*, pp. 140-141.

7. K. M. Panikkar argues that Ram Mohan Roy's study of Hebrew and Greek led him to the capacious vision of European liberalism: he rejected Christ, but he embraced 'the wide humanism of European thought, its ethics and its general approach to the problems of life'. He adds that as early as 1820 India embarked on her 'long adventure in building up a new civilization as a synthesis between the East and the West... and in that sense Ram Mohan is the forerunner of new India'.
    — *The Foundations of New India* (London: George Allen and Unwin, 1963), pp. 27-28. See also Panikkar's *Common Sense About India* (London: Victor Gollancz, 1960), pp. 20-21; and his *A Survey of Indian History* (London: Asia Publishing House, 1960 [1947]), pp. 214-215.

8. Max Müller's adulation of the Sanskrit tradition often broke the restraints of scholarship, reaching a somewhat hyperbolical pitch, as in one of his 1878 lectures in Westminster Abbey, 'The Ancient Literature of India':

    The number of separate works in Sanskrit, of which manuscripts are still in existence, is now estimated to amount to about 10,000. What would Aristotle have said, if he had been told that at his time there existed in India, in that India which Alexander had just discovered, if not conquered, an ancient literature far richer than anything existing at that time in Greece?
    — *Lectures on the Origin and Growth of Religion as Illustrated by the Religions of India* (London: Longmans, Green, & Co., 1882), p. 137. See also Appendix IV.

9.   F. Max Müller, *Biographical Essays* (London: Longmans, Green and Co., 1884), pp. 12-13.

10. Nirad C. Chaudhuri (1897-) recalls how Max Müller's legacy reached *his* consciousness, and why it stayed with him. He writes:

> My father was not a highly educated man in the formal sense, for he had received only a school education and that too in the backwaters of East Bengal and not in Calcutta, the centre of modern Bengali culture. Nonetheless, it was he who explained to me how Max Müller had established that our languages and the European languages belonged to the same family; that our words, *pita, mata, duhita,* etc., were the same as the English words, 'father', 'mother', 'daughter', etc.; that Sanskrit *Dyaus Pitr* and the Greek *Zeus Pater* were identical; and that we Hindus and the Europeans were both peoples descended from the same original stock. — *Scholar Extraordinary: The Life of Professor the Rt. Hon. Friedrich Max Müller, P.C.* (London: Chatto and Windus, 1974), p. 5.

11. Quoted in Jawaharlal Nehru, *The Discovery of India* (London: Meridian Books, 1956 [1946]), p. 77.

12. Tapan Raychaudhuri, *Europe Reconsidered: Perceptions of the West in Nineteenth Century Bengal* (Delhi: Oxford University Press, 1988), p 8.

13. Max Müller considered the *Rig Veda*, the first of the *Vedas*, the 'first word spoken by the Aryan man'. Nehru suggests that its antiquity surpasses the literature of Greece or Israel; indeed, that it is 'probably the earliest book that humanity possesses'; yet behind it, were 'ages of civilized existence'. The poet, Rabindranath Tagore, who won the Nobel Prize for Literature in 1913, has left us an enduring image of the inviolably pristine, touching, qualities of the Vedic hymns: '...a poetic testament of a people's collective reaction to the wonder and awe of existence. A people of vigorous and unsophisticated imagination awakened at the very dawn of civilisation to a sense of the inexhaustible mystery that is implicit in life. It was a simple faith of

theirs that attributed divinity to every element and force of nature, but it was a brave and joyous one, in which the sense of mystery only gave enchantment to life, without weighing it down with bafflement — the faith of a race unburdened with intellectual brooding on the conflicting diversity of the objective universe, though now and again illumined by intuitive experience...' See Nehru, *op. cit.*, [1956], pp. 65-69. (Tagore is quoted on p. 68).

14. The perspicacious Nehru regrets this lofty attribution; he settles for a more prosaic, but vastly illuminating, conception of the *Vedas*:

> The *Vedas*... were simply meant to be a collection of the existing knowledge of the day; they are a jumble of many things: hymns, prayers, ritual for sacrifice, magic, magnificent nature poetry. There is no idolatry in them; no temples for the gods. The vitality and affirmation of life pervading them are extraordinary. The early Vedic Aryans were so full of the zest for life that they paid little attention to the soul. In a vague way they believed in some kind of existence after death — *Ibid.*, p. 67.

15. Percival Spear argues that in spite of its austerity, reforming zeal, 'moral vigour', and 'pugnacious' attitude to Brahmanism, the impact of the *Arya Samaj* was greatly attenuated, because its 'modern outlook' on many issues was vitiated by its 'fundamentalist' assumptions. He concludes: '... many who were attracted by its anti-Brahmanism were repelled ... by its anti-rationalism'. — *The Oxford History of Modern India, 1740-1947* (Delhi: Oxford University Press, 1974 [1965]), p. 287.

16. For a fine scholarly assessment of Vivekananda's thoughts, and the intellectual and social environment which shaped his extraordinary mind, see Raychaudhuri, *op. cit.*, [1988].

17. Quoted in T. Walter Wallbank, *A Short History of India and Pakistan* (New York: The New American Library, 1965 [1958]), p. 101.

18. Nehru, *op. cit.*, [1956], p. 345.

19. Panikkar, *op. cit.*, [1963], p. 68. He adds: 'Without a Hindu ideology,

picturing the Hindu people as one, which Western scholarship and historiography enabled Hindus to create and develop, the alternative would have been the growth of regional nationalism based on recent and still remembered histories'. There would have been no Indian 'national' image. India would probably have balkanized into several linguistic and ethnic nations. — *Ibid.*, p. 69.

20. Quoted in *Nehru: The First Sixty Years, Vol. 1,* Dorothy Norman, (ed.), (London: The Bodley Head, 1965), p. 353.

21. Dwarka Nath, *A History of Indians in Guyana* (London: The Author, 1970 [1950]), p. 201.

22. Joseph Ruhomon was not a narrow Indian nationalist. As several of his pamphlets reveal, he was immersed in religious and philosophical speculation on questions of universal interest. See, for example, *Good and Evil, Signs and Portents,* and *Records of the Past.* (The only known copies of these pamphlets are located at the Caribbean Research Library, University of Guyana).

23. Peter Ruhomon, Joseph's younger brother, also read works on India, including Max Müller's. To underline the universal significance of the *Vedas,* he engaged the authority of Müller's *India: What it can Teach Us,* quoting thus:

> The Vedic Literature opens to us a chamber in the education of the human race to which we can find no parallel, anywhere else. Whoever cares for the historical growth of our language and thought, whoever cares for the first intelligible development of religion and mythology, whoever cares for the first foundation of Science, Astronomy, Metronomy, Grammar and Etymology, whoever cares for the first intimations of philosophical thoughts, for the first attempts at regulating family life, village life and state life as founded on religious ceremonials, traditions and contract, must, in future, pay full attention to the study of Vedic literature. — *Centenary History of the East Indians in British Guiana, 1838-1938* (Georgetown: East Indians 150th Anniver-

say Committee, 1988 [1947]), p. 261.

24. This author has been unable to locate any booklet or pamphlet, written by an Indian in the Caribbean, which predates Joseph Ruhomon's.

25. Ruhomon uses 'East Indians' to refer to Indians in British Guiana, as well as Indians in India and elsewhere. This classification was devised in British Guiana, to distinguish Indians from India and their descendants from the indigenous Indians, the Amerindians (American Indians).

26. Joseph Ruhomon, *India: The Progress of Her People at Home and Abroad, and How Those in British Guiana may Improve Themselves* (Georgetown: C. K. Jardine, 1894), p. 13.

27. *Ibid.*, pp. 8-9.

28. *The Berbice Gazette*, 27 January 1894.

29. *The Berbice Gazette*, 2 February 1895.

30. Joseph Ruhomon, *op. cit.*, [1894], p. 20.

31. *Ibid.*, p. 18.

32. *Ibid.*, p. 19. Ruhomon's use of 'Fatherland' is most unusual; India is always referred to as the 'Motherland' or 'Mother India' (*Bharata Mata*).

33. Romain Rolland, *The Life of Vivekananda and the Universal Gospel* (Calcutta: Advaita Ashrama, 1975 [1931]), p. 38.

34. Quoted in *Ibid.*., p. 40.

35. *Ibid.*, p. 37.

36. Joseph Ruhomon, *op. cit.*, [1894], p. 20.

37. *Ibid.*, p. 19.

38. *Ibid.*, p. 17.

39. *Ibid.*, p. 23.

40. *Ibid.*, p. 24.

41. *Ibid.*, p. 26.

42. Tyran Ramnarine, 'The Growth of the East Indian Community in British Guiana, 1880-1920', D. Phil. Thesis, University of Sussex, 1977, p. 268.

43. Nehru states that Vivekananda's celebration of *abhay* (fearlessness and strength), was 'the one constant refrain' of his speeches and writings. Vivekananda writes: 'If there is a sin in the world it is weakness; avoid all weakness, weakness is sin, weakness is death... anything that makes you weak physically, intellectually, and spiritually, reject as poison, there is no life in it, it cannot be true. Truth is strengthening'. He repudiated mysticism, which he considered weakening; and advocated a return to the *Upanishads*, 'the strengthening, the bright philosophy'. He rejected superstition as a genuflexion to weakness, an abrogation of life: 'I would rather see everyone of you rank atheists than superstitious fools, for the atheist is alive, and you can make something of him. But if superstition enters, the brain is gone, the brain is softening, degradation has seized upon the life'. — Quoted in Nehru, *op. cit.*, [1956], pp. 340-341.

44. Joseph Ruhomon, *op. cit.*, [1894], p. 25.

45. *Ibid.*, p. 29.

46. Joseph Ruhomon was instrumental in the formation of the British Guiana East Indian Association, in New Amsterdam, Berbice. At the inaugural meeting on 21 November 1916, he was elected secretary; his cousin, E. A. Luckhoo, a solicitor, was elected president. Ruhomon was the first editor of *Indian Opinion*, the organ of the Association. Only a couple of issues apparently appeared, before the Association became defunct. It was resuscitated in Georgetown, on 24 April 1919. — See *The Daily Chronicle*, 29 November 1916; Leader, *The Daily Chronicle*, 30 November 1916; Peter Ruhomon, *op. cit.*, [1988], pp. 234-237.

47. Joseph Ruhomon, *op. cit.*, [1894], pp. 28-29.

48. Veerasawmy Mudaliar [Vira Swami] was, for many years, the Chief Interpreter of the Immigration Department. In 1899, a Bengali resident of Calcutta, Gopi Nath Ghosh, wrote to *The Indian Mirror*, in India, extolling the achievements of Vira Swami (sic). This was a unique acknowledgement, in India, of an Indo-Guyanese. The letter

was reproduced in *The Argosy* [Georgetown], 25 May 1899:

> Mr. Swami... is one of the biggest landholders there (British Guiana). He is master of many thousands of dollars, and holds a most respected position in Damerara [sic] society. All this money he earned by his own extraordinary ability, ... his genial temper, and indomitable courage and energy. He is a self-made man in the true sense of the term. But the people of India are specially indebted to him for the great interest he takes in the Indian immigrants that have permanently settled in British Guiana or that go in hundreds from these shores every year... It is a shame that we do not know such men even by name, men who are silently working for our countrymen and women in some of the remotest corners of the world. It is a pity we lose touch with such men as Mr. Swami... For our own fault, we have lost these bold and energetic colonists of our country — who feel for us, who have the greatest love for their mother-country, and who are always eager to shake us by the hand as brethren across the seas.

49. This historic event was reported thus in the local press: 'An interesting figure in the next Parliament will be the Parsee, Naoroji, whom Lord Salisbury (the Tory Leader), held up to mistaken ridicule as a 'black man'. His return in Central Finsbury, by three votes, was challenged by the Conservatives, but a recount confirmed Naoroji's poll'. — *The Daily Chronicle*, 28 July 1892.

50. As late as November 1916, *The Daily Chronicle*, while applauding the 'most remarkable strides' of the 'thrifty and industrious' Indo-Guyanese, noted their 'scant influence', their 'very unpretentious' role, in the public life of the colony. The paper elaborated: '... as a race they have been content to concentrate their attention upon the task of improving their status in the community, and have been content to hold themselves aloof from those more conscious aspirations which would have brought them within the glare of the limelight ...'

— Leader, *The Daily Chronicle*, 30 November 1916.

51. This biographical sketch of Dr. Wharton is constructed from his entry in *Who is Who in British Guiana, 1945-1948* (Georgetown: The Daily Chronicle Ltd., 1948), pp. 551-552.

52. Rozina Visram, *Ayahs, Lascars and Princes: Indians in Britain, 1700-1947* (London: Pluto Press, 1986), p. 181.

53. See note 51.

54. Nirad C. Chaudhuri, *op. cit.*, [1974], p. 185.

55. *Ibid.*, p. 1. Steven Vertovec argues that Max Müller's work in Indology acquired national recognition in Britain as well: 'He edited, and persuaded the Oxford University Press to publish a series of sacred books of the past. His enthusiastic assertion of the common Aryan origins of Indians and Anglo-Saxons and his sympathy for Indian culture made his home in Oxford a place of pilgrimage for many Indians visiting England... The latter part of the nineteenth century was something of a golden age, when Max Mueller's [sic] books made Indian studies fashionable, not only in Oxford, but in the country as a whole, and even Queen Victoria had her *munshi* [Indian teacher]'. Vertovec, 'Indian Studies at Oxford', in *Oxford University Papers on India, Vol. 2, Part 2: Aspects of the South Asian Diaspora*, Vertovec, (ed.), (Delhi: Oxford University Press, 1991), pp. xii — xiii, xv.

56. Joseph Ruhomon, *op. cit.*, [1894], pp. 20-21.

57. Leader, *The Daily Chronicle*, 8 September 1892.

58. Leader, *The Argosy*, 12 September 1891.

59. Nirad C. Chaudhuri, *op. cit.*, [1974], p. 318. Chaudhuri quotes Vivekananda's tribute to Max Müller's communion with ancient and modern India: 'There are a number of great souls in the West who undoubtedly are well-wishers of India, but I am not aware of one in Europe who is a greater well-wisher. He is not only a well-wisher, but also a deep believer in Indian philosophy and religion... Though all through his life he has lived with and steeped himself in ancient Sanskrit literature, the India of the Professor's imagination is not sim-

ply that which resounded with the chanting of the Vedas and from which sacrificial smoke rose to the sky... he also is ever alert to whatever in the way of new developments is happening in every corner of India and keeps himself well-posted about them'. — *Ibid.*, p. 5.

60. This was done by the British Guiana East Indian Institute, possibly the first Indian Society in the Caribbean. — Peter Ruhomon, *op. cit.*, [1988], p. 234.

61. J. R.Wharton, an Indo-Guyanese solicitor and brother of Dr. William Hewley Wharton, 'initiated and successfully carried out the project of forwarding an illuminated address from the Indian inhabitants of this colony to George V, on his accession to the throne'. In 1892, he was instrumental in sending an 'illuminated address of congratulations', through the East Indian Institute, to Dadabhai Naoroji, the first Indian M. P. in Britain. — *The Daily Argosy*, 15 September 1922.

62. Quoted in A. L. Basham, *The Wonder that was India: A Survey of the History and Culture of the Indian Sub-Continent before the Coming of the Muslims* (London: Fontana/Collins, 1971 [1954]), p. 87.

63. This poem was first published in the local press in January 1901. It was reproduced in *Anthology of Local Indian Verse*, C. E. J. Ramcharitar-Lalla, (ed.), (Georgetown: 'The Argosy' Co., 1934), pp. 27-29. It was recently republished in *Offerings*, Kampta Karran, (ed.), No. 9, (September 1991), pp. 8-9.

64. The cases of Parmanand and Sharma are discussed in Ramnarine, *op. cit.*, [1977], pp. 243-244.

65. *The Daily Chronicle*, 29 August 1916.

66. *Ibid.*

67. Quoted in B. R. Nanda, *Gokhale: The Indian Moderate and the British Raj*, (Delhi: Oxford University Press, 1977), p. 446.

68. Visram, *op. cit.*, [1986], p. 116; Robert G. Gregory, *India and East Africa: A History of Race Relations Within the British Empire, 1890-1939* (Oxford: Clarendon Press, 1971), pp. 146-148.

69. Leader, *The Daily Argosy*, 8 February 1916.

70.   Ramcharitar-Lalla, *op. cit.*, [1934], p. 12.

71.   Percival Spear, *op. cit.*, [1974], p. 341.

72.   'M. K. Gandhi to the Viceroy ...', 1 August 1920', in *The Indian Nationalist Movement, 1885-1947: Select Documents*, B. N. Pandey, (ed.), (London: Macmillan, 1979), p. 53.

73.   *The Daily Argosy*, 25 February 1920.

74.   *Ibid.*

75.   On his return to British Guiana, the Governor, Sir Wilfred Collet (the Bill was introduced during his absence), informed the Colonial Office that '...many people, including Government officials, have a wrong idea of what is meant by sedition'. And, with rare objectivity, he observed: 'There seems to be some kind of idea amongst certain people, that when black people make complaints, this is seditious, but it is not if complaints are made by Europeans'. — C. O. [Colonial Office] 111/630, Collet to Milner, confidential, 14 April 1920.

   But reason soon deserted Collet. In April 1922, he reported to the Colonial Office that the delegates from India, Pillai and Tivary, were 'present at a number of meetings that might fairly be called seditious'. They were simply meeting Indians in the course of their inquiry. — C. O. 111/643, Collet to Churchill, No. 164, 28 April 1922.

76.   *The Daily Argosy*, 4 March 1920.

77.   J. A. Luckhoo, 'The East Indians in British Guiana', *Timehri*, Vol. vi, (third series), (1919), pp. 64-65.

78.   The Reports of these delegates are invaluable documents on the Indian condition in British Guiana in the 1920s. See the following: *Reports on the Scheme for Indian Emigration to British Guiana, Part 1 — Report by Dewan Bahadur P. Kesava Pillai and V. N. Tivary...* (Simla: Government Press, 1924); Report by Kunwar Maharaj Singh on His Deputation to British Guiana in 1925; C.F. Andrews, *An Interim Statement Concerning East Indian Conditions in British Guiana* (Georgetown: The Daily Chronicle Ltd., 1929); C. F. Andrews, 'Impressions of British Guiana', (mimeo.). — C. O. 111/689/75141 [1930], enclosure.

79. For a detailed discussion of this complicated scheme and the myriad, underlying issues in which it became entangled, see my 'An Indian Colony Aborted?: The British Guiana Colonisation Scheme, 1919-1929', (mimeo.).

80. I. O. L/E/7/1254 — J. & P. 5169/1919, encl. No. 4 [India Office Library and Records].

81. The call for an Indian Colony was repeated in a pamphlet written by J. A. Luckhoo and Dr. William Hewley Wharton. This pamphlet, *British Guiana Imperial Colonization Scheme*, was published in 1919, in London, controversially under the name of the British Guiana East Indian Association. Luckhoo and Wharton wrote: 'The resident Indians in British Guiana would like to embrace the opportunity now offered by the Government to make British Guiana an Indian Colony. They would like to encourage the settlement in the Colony of Indians of every class and trade. At present the labouring and agricultural classes can materially improve their general condition by emigrating to the Colony, and would, in a short time, be able to amass sufficient competence to make them fairly independent'. — C. O. 111/636, (Nunan), 24 March 1920, encl.

82. Leader, *The Daily Argosy*, 21 December 1920.

83. Leader, *The Daily Argosy*, 18 January 1921.

84. *The Daily Argosy*, 15 March 1922.

85. Leader, *The Daily Argosy*, 11 July 1923.

86. *The Daily Chronicle*, 24 March 1922.

87. *The Daily Argosy*, 6 February 1925.

88. See *The Daily Argosy*, 8 March 1925, for Alfred Ramsing's letter of 7 March 1925 and Lupton's reply.

89. Leader, *The Daily Argosy*, 30 June 1926.

90. *The Daily Argosy*, 25 June 1929.

91. Leader, *The Daily Argosy*, 27 March 1929.

92. Leader, *The New Daily Chronicle*, 26 July 1927.

93. 'De Omnibus Rebus' [by the Editor], *The New Daily Chronicle*, 14

August 1927.

94. See my *Indians in British Guiana, 1919-1929...*, *op. cit.*, Chapter 4, Part IV — Creolised Indians and the Shaping of an Intellectual Vision: The [Wesleyan] East Indian Young Men's Society (E.I.Y.M.S.).

95. *The Daily Chronicle*, 12 October 1919.

96. The following are some of the other lectures on India, delivered to the Society in the 1920s:

Lecturer	Topic	Where Cited
Madhoo Lal Bose	Impressions of India	*The Daily Argosy*, 15 May 1920
J. A. Luckhoo	The Future of India	*do.*, 26 August 1920
Deva Ram Sokul	Rabindranath Tagore: The Poet and his Message	*do.*, 6 January 1921
V. N. Tivary	Young Indians and Social Service	*do.*, 21 February 1922
Rev. Stanley Edwards	Impressions of India	*The Daily Chronicle*, 9 March 1922
Rev. Wm. Mackin	Six Kings of India	*The Daily Argosy* 20 March 1925
Staff Capt. Hackett	India	*The New Daily Chronicle*, 5 June 1927
Peter Ruhomon	Christ in Relation to India	*The Daily Argosy*, 19 June 1927
Mehta Jaimini	The Fundamental Basis of Religion	*do.*, 14 May 1929

97. *The Daily Chronicle*, 9 March 1922.

98. *The Daily Argosy*, 11 February 1923.

99. *The Daily Argosy*, 30 October 1925.

100. *Ibid..* In mid-1929, C. F. Andrews observed of Indo-Guyanese women: they 'are very free in their movements from one place to another in British Guiana. They have a healthy out-of-door existence and there is no seclusion'. — C. O. 111/689/75141 [1930], 'Im-

pressions of British Guiana', (mimeo.), p. 75.

101. *The New Daily Chronicle*, 30 June 1927.

102. It is refreshing to read the enlightened views of several Indian men on the education of Indo-Guianese women. In October 1936, for instance, H. S. G. Sampat of No 57 Village, Corentyne, in an open letter to the Indians of British Guiana, called up ancient Indian history in making his case:

> ... the ancient Aryan race... were a great people, because their women were highly educated. Their high attainments in every department of knowledge can be seen from the fact that some of the most beautiful hymns of the *Rig Veda* were written by women. As soon as this system of education began to decline, the development of our once powerful civilization commenced to deteriorate. — *The Daily Chronicle*, 18 October 1936.

103. *The Daily Argosy*, 5 April 1929.

104. Jeremy Poynting, 'At Homes, Tagore and Jive: Ethnic Identity and the British Guiana Dramatic Society', *Kyk-over-al*, No. 37, (December 1987), p. 48.

105. *The New Daily Chronicle*, 2 September 1926.

106. See the *Wesleyan Methodist Missionary Society Reports, vol. xxxv (1918-1922): The One Hundred and Fifth Report of the W.M.M.S. (1918); The One Hundred and Sixth Report of the W.M.M.S. (1919)* (These, as well as the M.M.S. archives, are housed at SOAS Library, University of London).

Rev. Yates reported that in 1919, Pandit Ramsaroop was brought before the Council of the Hindu temple at Albouystown, and a demand was made that he should withdraw permission from the Methodists for use of the building he had loaned them, 'with the object of driving us from the neighbourhood'. Ramsaroop replied: 'God told me to give the Church to the Methodists. When He tells me to take it from them I will, but not until then. You can kill me if you like. I go by His orders'. — *The One Hundred and Sixth Report of* the *W.M.M.S. (1919)*, pp. 83-84.

107. See note 105.

108. *Ibid..*

109. *The New Daily Chronicle*, 17 August 1926.

110. *The Daily Argosy*, 16 July 1929.

111. Peter Ruhomon, *op. cit.*, [1988], p. 253.

112. *The Daily Chronicle*, 2 December 1941.

113. In the late 1930s, Peter Ruhomon noted that there were over fifty mosques in British Guiana; but the Queenstown mosque, 'with its triple silvered domes, glistening in the morning sunrise or reflecting the level rays of the setting sun, stands unique among them, in its graceful proportions and unadorned simplicity...' — *Ibid.*, p. 267.

114. In a lecture to the British Guiana East Indian Association, on 2 March 1920, Mungal Singh, an Indo-Guyanese lawyer, underlined the pain occasioned by the use of the 'opprobious' term, 'coolie'. It was 'flashed and dashed about indiscriminately'; and, often to the '[Indians'] indignation, flaunted in the faces of ladies and gentlemen'. Mungal Singh felt that legislation should be introduced to eradicate the pejorative term; and that Indians who felt outraged when called a 'coolie', should seek legal redress. — *The Daily Argosy*, 27 March 1920.

115. In Trinidad, also, where Jaimini delivered about eighty lectures, he fired the imagination and pride of the Indians. Beatrice Greig, a British woman residing in Trinidad, an avid supporter of Indian nationalism, recalled Jaimini's commanding performance in a lecture in Port-of-Spain in December 1928: he had a 'brilliant brain', 'prodigious memory', 'burning enthusiasm', and a 'strong clear voice'; he claimed their attention for two hours, remaining 'so fresh and sustained that he could have continued for another hour with unimpaired vigour'. For Greig, it was a magisterial exhibition: 'His mind stored with the truths of ancient wisdom, the words of some of the greatest European writers on his lips. Expounding the man-

tras of that great Hindu poem 'The Vedas' as they have never been revealed in Trinidad before, and arousing in all who heard him that pride of race that must inevitably lift them to a higher intellectual and spiritual level...' — 'India Section', *The Beacon* [Trinidad], Vol. 2, No. ii, (June 1932), pp. 35-36.

116. *The Daily Argosy*, 26 March 1929.

117. *The Daily Argosy*, 29 May 1929.

118. *The Daily Argosy*, 17 May 1929.

119. *The Daily Argosy*, 8 May 1929.

120. For an ongoing coverage of Andrews's sojourn in British Guiana, see the following issues of *The Daily Argosy*: 18, 19, 22, 24, 28 May 1929; 5, 9, 13, 14, 16, 18, 25 June 1929; 7, 16 July 1929; 21 August 1929.

121. *The Daily Argosy*, 28 May 1929.

122. Leader, *The Daily Argosy*, 27 March 1929. Lupton's editorial was in response to Mehta Jaimini's erudite lecture, to a mixed audience, at the Town Hall, Georgetown. He observed that Jaimini 'expounded the tenets of the Brahmo Samaj rather than the Arya Samaj, with excursions into the Tolstoyism ... which form the inspiration of Mr. Gandhi': he was 'obviously not a militant nationalist'. Lupton noted that Jaimini was 'welcomed fraternally by Muslim and Hindu alike'; and that British Guiana had a lesson to teach India — 'the lesson of religious tolerance and of brotherhood among those of the Indian races that live so amicably in out midst...'

123. *The Daily Argosy*, 6 May 1938.

124. *The Daily Argosy*, 7 March 1922.

125. *The Daily Chronicle*, 1 April 1922.

126. See my *Indians in British Guiana, 1919-1929...*, *op. cit.*, Chapter 2, Part VI — The Ruimveldt Killings of 1924.

127. See note 121.

128. *Ibid.*.

129. C. O. 950/941, (West India Royal Commission, 1938-1939, Written Evidence, Vol. 3).

130. *The New Daily Chronicle*, 7 August 1927.

131. I. O. L. — E. & O. 5135/1927, Edun to Polak, 2 September 1927, encl. [India Office Library and Records].

132. *Ibid.*

133. *Ibid.*

134. *Ibid.*

135. I. O. L. — E. & O. 5135/1927, British Guiana East Indian Association to the Officer Administering the Government, C. Douglas-Jones, 3 January 1928.

136. Quoted in Hugh Tinker, *Separate and Unequal: India and the Indians in the British Commonwealth, 1920-1950* (London: C Hurst and Co., 1976), p. 93.

137. Quoted in Robert G. Gregory, *op. cit.*, [1971], p. 410.

138. *The Daily Chronicle*, 30 October 1936.

139. Nehru, *op. cit.*,[1956], p. 55.

Index of Names, Newspapers, Organisations and Selected Books